MARGARET ATWOOD

Critical Companions to Popular Contemporary Writers
Second Series

Isabel Allende *by Karen Castellucci Cox*

Julia Alvarez *by Silvio Sirias*

Rudolfo A. Anaya *by Margarite Fernandez Olmos*

Maya Angelou *by Mary Jane Lupton*

Ray Bradbury *by Robin Anne Reid*

Revisiting Mary Higgins Clark *by Linda De Roche*

Louise Erdrich *by Lorena L. Stookey*

Ernest J. Gaines *by Karen Carmean*

Gabriel García Márquez *by Rubén Pelayo*

Kaye Gibbons *by Mary Jean DeMarr*

John Irving *by Josie P. Campbell*

Garrison Keillor *by Marcia Songer*

Jamaica Kincaid *by Lizabeth Paravisini-Gebert*

Revisiting Stephen King *by Sharon A. Russell*

Barbara Kingsolver *by Mary Jean DeMarr*

Maxine Hong Kingston *by E. D. Huntley*

Terry McMillan *by Paulette Richards*

Larry McMurtry *by John M. Reilly*

Toni Morrison *by Missy Dehn Kubitschek*

Walter Mosley *by Charles E. Wilson, Jr.*

Gloria Naylor *by Charles E. Wilson, Jr.*

James Patterson *by Joan G. Kotker*

Chaim Potok *by Sanford Sternlicht*

Amy Tan *by E. D. Huntley*

Anne Tyler *by Paul Bail*

Leon Uris *by Kathleen Shine Cain*

Kurt Vonnegut *by Thomas F. Marvin*

James Welch *by Mary Jane Lupton*

Tom Wolfe *by Brian Abel Ragen*

MARGARET ATWOOD

A Critical Companion

Nathalie Cooke

CRITICAL COMPANIONS TO POPULAR CONTEMPORARY WRITERS
Kathleen Gregory Klein, Series Editor

Greenwood Press
Westport, Connecticut • London

Library of Congress Cataloging-in-Publication Data

Cooke, Nathalie.
    Margaret Atwood : a critical companion / Nathalie Cooke.
       p. cm. — (Critical companions to popular contemporary writers, ISSN 1082–4979)
    Includes bibliographical references and index.
    ISBN 0–313–32806–4
       1. Atwood, Margaret Eleanor, 1939—Criticism and interpretation—Handbooks,
manuals, etc.   2. Women and literature—Canada—History—20th century—Handbooks,
manuals, etc.   I. Title. II. Series.
  PR9199.3.A8Z573 2004
  813'.54—dc22   2004012231

British Library Cataloguing in Publication Data is available.

Library of Congress Catalog Card Number: 2004012231
ISBN: 0–313–32806–4
ISSN: 1082–4979

First published in 2004

Greenwood Press, 88 Post Road West, Westport, CT 06881
An imprint of Greenwood Publishing Group, Inc.
www.greenwood.com

Printed in the United States of America

The paper used in this book complies with the
Permanent Paper Standard issued by the National
Information Standards Organization (Z39.48–1984).

10 9 8 7 6 5 4 3 2 1

Copyright Acknowledgment

Shelley Boyd quote of King Lear passage is reprinted with permission of Shelley Boyd.

Contents

Series Foreword

The authors who appear in the series Critical Companions to Popular Contemporary Writers are all best-selling writers. They do not simply have one successful novel, but a string of them. Fans, critics, and specialist readers eagerly anticipate their next book. For some, high cash advances and breakthrough sales figures are automatic; movie deals often follow. Some writers become household names, recognized by almost everyone.

But, their novels are read one by one. Each reader chooses to start and, more importantly, to finish a book because of what she or he finds there. The real test of a novel is in the satisfaction its readers experience. This series acknowledges the extraordinary involvement of readers and writers in creating a best-seller.

The authors included in this series were chosen by an Advisory Board composed of high school English teachers and high school and public librarians. They ranked a list of best-selling writers according to their popularity among different groups of readers. For the first series, writers in the top-ranked group who had received no book-length, academic, literary analysis (or none in at least the past ten years) were chosen. Because of this selection method, Critical Companions to Popular Contemporary Writers meets a need that is being addressed nowhere else. The success of these volumes as reported by reviewers, librarians, and teachers led to an expansion of the series mandate to include some writers with wide critical attention—Toni Morrison, John Irving, and Maya Angelou, for example—to extend the usefulness of the series.

The volumes in the series are written by scholars with particular expertise in analyzing popular fiction. These specialists add an academic focus to the popular success that these writers already enjoy.

The series is designed to appeal to a wide range of readers. The general reading public will find explanations for the appeal of these well-known writers. Fans will find biographical and fictional questions answered. Students will find literary analysis, discussions of fictional genres, carefully organized introductions to new ways of reading the novels, and bibliographies for additional research. Whether browsing through the book for pleasure or using it for an assignment, readers will find that the most recent novels of the authors are included.

Each volume begins with a biographical chapter drawing on published information, autobiographies or memoirs, prior interviews, and, in some cases, interviews given especially for this series. A chapter on literary history and genres describes how the author's work fits into a larger literary context. The following chapters analyze the writer's most important, most popular, and most recent novels in detail. Each chapter focuses on one or more novels. This approach, suggested by the Advisory Board as the most useful to student research, allows for an in-depth analysis of the writer's fiction. Close and careful readings with numerous examples show readers exactly how the novels work. These chapters are organized around three central elements: plot development (how the story line moves forward), character development (what the reader knows of the important figures), and theme (the significant ideas of the novel). Chapters may also include sections on generic conventions (how the novel is similar or different from others in its same category of science fiction, fantasy, thriller, etc.), narrative point of view (who tells the story and how), symbols and literary language, and historical or social context. Each chapter ends with an "alternative reading" of the novel. The volume concludes with a primary and secondary bibliography, including reviews.

The alternative readings are a unique feature of this series. By demonstrating a particular way of reading each novel, they provide a clear example of how a specific perspective can reveal important aspects of the book. In the alternative reading sections, one contemporary literary theory—way of reading, such as feminist criticism, Marxism, new historicism, deconstruction, or Jungian psychological critique—is defined in brief, easily comprehensible language. That definition is then applied to the novel to highlight specific features that might go unnoticed or be understood differently in a more general reading. Each volume defines two or three specific theories, making them part of the reader's understanding of how diverse meanings may be constructed from a single novel.

Taken collectively, the volumes in the Critical Companions to Popular Contemporary Writers series provide a wide-ranging investigation of the complexities of current best-selling fiction. By treating these novels seriously as both literary works and publishing successes, the series demonstrates the potential of popular literature in contemporary culture.

Kathleen Gregory Klein
Southern Connecticut State University

1

A Brief Biography of
Margaret Atwood

One brief digression in Atwood's book *Negotiating with the Dead: A Writer on Writing* is particularly revealing about Atwood's writing technique and, indeed, about why her work is so wildly appealing to audiences. Within a larger discussion of the way art has been perceived and valued through the ages, and a more focused discussion of censorship in the twentieth century, she interjects a few comments on what the atmosphere of the late 1950s was *really* like—from the point of view of a young woman. It was a time when you couldn't "buy contraceptives over the counter, and you couldn't buy them at all if you were an unmarried woman," a time when you couldn't "get an abortion except somewhere else," a time when sanitary napkins were advertised on the television without the product ever actually being named, which "gave rise to a degree of surrealism unmatched in advertising since" (76–77). No wonder that, as she admits, Atwood had no idea about what they were discussing in Hemingway's "Hills like White Elephants" when she first read it. Abortion was something that people did not speak about.

Precisely what this excerpt reveals is how Atwood makes the issues of the day—the politics of her times and her profession (censorship, feminism, sexuality)—compelling: by making them personal, sometimes so idiosyncratically personal that they are funny. Atwood's writing attests to the power of the first-person pronoun, "I," and what an individual sees with her own "eyes." "Writers," explains Atwood, "are eye-witnesses, I-witnesses" (*Second Words* 203). For example, the central character in *The Edible Woman*, Marian, experiences the symptoms of anorexia nervosa when she develops a problematic relationship with the items on her own plate. In *Surfacing*, the Surfacer really recognizes the threat of the Americanization of Canada when she resists selling her recently deceased parents' property to a land developer. Offred, one of the few fertile women in the Gileadean society of *The Handmaid's Tale*, can speak to the negative effects of pollution because she sees, every day, how it has affected those around her. Snowman, in *Oryx and Crake*, has something to say about the practical implications of genetically modified plants and animals.

Again and again in her writing, Atwood revitalizes the stories with which we are familiar by telling them from a personal, and refreshingly original, point of view. In the poem "Miss July Grows Older," from *Morning in the Burned House*, we hear from the magazine centerfold. In "Gertrude Talks Back," from *Good Bones*, we finally hear from Hamlet's mother. Among other things, she regrets agreeing to name her son Hamlet: "[a]ll those terrible jokes about pork" (15). In *The Blind Assassin*, I shall argue that we seem to hear one of the stories of classic Greek tragedy told from the sister's point of view. In "Marrying the Hangman," from *Two-Headed Poems*, we hear straight from the female prisoner how she convinced the man in the cell next to her to become the hangman and then to marry her. In "Siren Song," one of the Songs of the Transformed from *You Are Happy*, we hear the most intimate secret of all: what the siren sang to lure her victims to their deaths.

Atwood uses the same technique to bring history to life. In *The Journals of Susanna Moodie*, it is Susanna who describes what it feels like to be a genteel Englishwoman in Canada's nineteenth-century bush. In *Alias Grace*, Grace talks about the kind of historical details that seldom make it into the history books: what life is like from the servant girl's point of view, as well as what it is like from a prisoner's point of view. In "The Bombardment Continues," in *Story of a Nation: Defining Moments in Our History*, Atwood describes the siege of Quebec from the point of view of one woman, Marie Payzant.

If Atwood renders politics personal, surely it is no wonder that readers are fascinated about how her personal life translates into the politics of her writing. In some ways, then, Atwood's writing technique actually invites readers' scrutiny of biographical details of her life.

Readers can find out quite a bit about Atwood's life. Two full-length biographies were published in 1998: *The Red Shoes, Atwood Starting Out*, which ends in 1976, and my own, *Margaret Atwood: A Biography*, which traces her life until the publication of *Alias Grace* in 1996. As well, there have been a number of commentaries tracing particular aspects of her life and career; these include commentaries by Atwood herself, sections of Jerome Rosenberg's 1984 book called *Margaret Atwood* and of Coral Ann Howells's 1996 book of the same name, as well as my own article summarizing the different biographical approaches taken to date, "Lions, Tigers, and Pussycats: Margaret Atwood [Auto-]Biographically." Together, these provide a relatively complete discussion of the way Atwood's upbringing, education, and early formation as a writer provided a foundation for the direction of her writing, particularly its central themes of environmental awareness, Canadian nationalism, and feminism.

However, Atwood's writing reflects a fourth preoccupation—with the writer's craft—particularly with writers' ability to weave the dark mysteries of fiction or to dispel those mysteries as merely fictional. In her own work, Atwood does both. Generally, this preoccupation with the writer's craft is discussed by critical commentators in terms of the "gothic" (Davison) and "satiric" aspects of her writing. In this study, the dark and mysterious or "gothic" elements are discussed in relation to Atwood's earlier novels (*Surfacing* and *Lady Oracle*), and the "satiric" elements are introduced in the discussion of Atwood's earliest novel (*The Edible Woman*) and then traced in Atwood's later novels as the impulse behind their challenges to character in the artist novels, setting in the dystopic fiction, and plot in the villainess novels.

In what follows, I will trace some of the sources of the ecological, nationalist, and feminist impulses in Atwood's work and offer some suggestions about what might drive her fascination with the writer and the writer's vocation.

ECOLOGICAL CONCERNS

Atwood's focus on ecological awareness can be traced to her father and the lifestyle he established for his family. Atwood's father came from the Maritimes, near Shelburne, Nova Scotia. One of five children, he finished high school through correspondence courses, began teaching at the age of 16, and attended university on scholarship. He was a forest entomologist and professor of Zoology at the University of Toronto who took his family into the bush each summer, where he set up a forest workstation and the family set up camp in a tent. His research focused on the spruce budworm, and he was one of the first to suggest that spraying would not work to control the budworm population. Carl Atwood was a fine woodsman, capable of single-handedly building the family cabin (interview with author). This cabin, which forms the basis of the setting for *Surfacing* and is captured by Michael Rubbo in his 1984 film, was not completed until Atwood was 27 and still has neither phone nor running water. A friend of the well-known and well-respected woodsman M. T. Kelly, Carl Atwood figures in a number of the family stories about camping. He was the one who survived a forest fire, trapped in a tent with three others (fortunately) in the middle of a rainstorm. He was the one who stretched his university scholarship money by staying in a tent for part of the year and cleaning rabbit hutches to earn a bit of extra money. He was the one M. T. Kelly asked for advice when he was about to buy a gun. Atwood glowed with pride the day she told me about her father, "one-match Atwood" (interview with author).

Carl Atwood suffered a transitory stroke while driving on the 401 just north of Toronto in March 1992. It is described, accurately, in the story "In Search of the Rattlesnake Plantain," included in the American edition of *Bluebeard's Egg*, entitled *Bluebeard's Egg and Other Stories.* Such an accurate portrayal of Atwood's family in her fiction was strikingly unusual and, as Atwood admitted later, a conscious "answer to people who mistakenly thought the heroine's parents in *Surfacing* were pictures of [her] own parents" (in Lyons, "Dreadful Childhoods" 225). While the stroke only affected the use of Carl Atwood's left hand, it signaled a decline that would lead to his death in January of 1993. Contained within *Morning in the Burned House,* itself a poetry collection exploring personal and cultural memory, is a moving sequence of poems devoted to Atwood's father, the man who "carried the green canoe" (95), the same man who, in the narrative present of these poems, no longer has use of his left hand or full use of his two feet (88).

Born in Ottawa in 1939, Atwood spent her early childhood, from the age of six months, moving to the bush in the summer and back to a variety of Canada's urban centers in the winter: Sudbury, Sault Sainte Marie, Ottawa, and then Toronto. She would not spend a full year in the city until she was eight. Although she, like her father, has ultimately settled in Canada's largest city, Toronto, there were two significant periods when Atwood lived in rural or wilderness settings. The first was during her summers as a camp counselor. The second time was when, in the early 1970s, after Atwood's resignation from Anansi Press and after the publication of *Surfacing* and *Survival* and the media frenzy that, as Atwood described it, transformed her from an individual to a "thing" ("Getting out from Under"), Atwood and her partner Graeme Gibson moved to the relative peace of Beeton, Ontario, where they rented a farm in 1973, and then to Alliston, Ontario, where they bought one. Here, Atwood collected mail once a week from her post box in Alliston and worked in a room from which she didn't have to listen to the phone ringing. She and Gibson started a vegetable garden, eventually won the war against garden slugs, and came to know the names of all the various forms of weeds. A number of Atwood's poems date from this time, some obviously drawn from the couple's daily experiences, like "The Bus to Alliston, Ontario" in *Two-Headed Poems,* and others inspired by the figures around them, like the various Songs of the Transformed in *You Are Happy.* Some of the best-known works from this time—*Lady Oracle,* and the powerful poem and story that can be seen as early sketches for it, "Tricks with Mirrors" (in *You Are Happy)* and "The Man from Mars" (from *Dancing Girls*) respectively—have little to do with the rural Alliston landscape.

When Atwood returns to focus on the wilderness in her fiction, most obviously in stories like "Death by Landscape" and "The Age of Lead" in *Wilderness Tips* (1991), it seems to draw her back to the landscapes of her younger years as a camp counselor. After grade 12, for example, she worked in the Crippled Children's Camp, which is depicted in "Training," a story in *Dancing Girls;* and after grade 13, she worked as a waitress at Camp Hurontario, which inspires "True Trash" in *Wilderness Tips.* What prompted this return to the natural landscape, I expect, was a genuine sense that it was being threatened. In a 1987 article, she speaks out against pollution and the encroachment of civilization, and in defense of the loon and what the loon symbolizes to Canadians: clean lakes ("True North" 148). The loon, for those who have never had the blessing of seeing or hearing one, is the dark bird with a distinctive white collar and laugh-like call that is immortalized on the Canadian one-dollar coin, itself familiarly known as the "loonie." However, it was really Camp White Pine in Haliburton, about two-and-a-half hours northeast of Toronto, where Atwood spent three summers as a counselor, that seems to have played the most significant role in shaping her developing activism and extending her network of contacts. At White Pine, Atwood came to know a number of talented individuals who would play an important role on the Canadian artistic scene, including three who would become close friends and artistic collaborators: the editor and writer Rick Salutin, for whom Atwood would later provide articles under her own name and cartoons under the pseudonym Bart Gerrard for publication in *This Magazine;* artist Charles Pachter, who would later illustrate a number of Atwood's books; and Beryl Fox, of the television program *This Hour Has Seven Days* and the Vietnam documentary *The Mills of the Gods*. Pachter recalls that "Peggy Nature," as she was nicknamed, looked rather like Jane Goodall in those camp days: "rubber boots, shorts, maybe even a machete at the side, 'shmata' on her head" during her time as Nature Counselor (interview with the author, 8 Sept 1995).

As well, at White Pine, a reform Jewish camp, Atwood became sensitized to issues touching Jews after World War II. One man, she recalls, "had a number on his arm" and did nothing but peel potatoes in the White Pine kitchen (in Atwood, "The Empress" 182). Although Atwood's own work makes only a few references to the Holocaust (as when Offred remembers a televised interview with the mistress of a concentration camp supervisor just as she assumes a similar position in becoming the Commander's mistress), the reverberations of man's inhumanity to man, which is ultimately what the Holocaust comes to represent in the post–WWII period, can be felt throughout her oeuvre. Indeed, Atwood's commitment to human rights issues has led to her direct involvement in PEN Canada and PEN International, an organization that works on behalf of silenced writers around the world in pursuit of freedom of expression. The protection of human rights is the implicit subject of her dystopian fiction, and it is the explicit subject of "A Travel Piece" (in *Dancing Girls*), *Bodily Harm*, and *True Stories* (particularly the section "Notes towards a Poem That Can Never Be Written"). All three were prompted by two trips: one to Portland, in which Atwood had a discussion with poet Carolyn Forché, to whom *True Stories* is dedicated, about the situation in El Salvador; and another to Saint Vincent, where locals came, "under the cover of night," to tell Atwood their stories of horror (in Atwood, "Witness is What You Must Bear" 164). Readers interested in pursuing the details of Atwood's political activism should look particularly at "Amnesty International: An Address" in *Second Words*. On the subject of man's inhumanity to man, and in particular the individual's potential for cruelty, readers might look at "It is Dangerous to Read Newspapers" from *The Animals in That Country*, as well as "Trainride, Vienna-Bonn" from *True Stories*.

FEMINIST CONCERNS

If the lifestyle established by Atwood's father raised her consciousness about ecological awareness, then her mother's family modeled possibilities for women beyond the roles generally available to women of Atwood's own generation. Their ancestress, the seventeenth-century Puritan Mary Webster, of the poem "Half-Hanged Mary" and of the same family as Noah Webster of dictionary fame, is emblematic of the strength of the Killam women. Atwood explains how Mary was hanged as a witch in Connecticut "for 'causing an old man to become extremely valetudinarious.' . . . When they cut Mary Webster down the next day, she was, to everyone's surprise, not dead." The punch line of the story has to do with Mary Webster's "tough neck" (*Second Words* 331). In reality, Mary's luck had more to do with the fact that they had not yet invented "the drop," and so her neck was not actually broken in the hanging (in Atwood, "Witch Craft" 28). However, the point of the story still applies: having a tough neck was a valuable thing for a woman then, and it remains a valuable legacy for the Killam women who followed her.

In Atwood's immediate family, there are three formidable Killam ancestors: her mother Margaret, who spent summers in the bush, literally kept the campfires burning, and took up ice dancing later in life (see "Woman Skating" in *Procedures for Underground*); her Aunt Kay Cogswell, who graduated with an MA in History from the University of Toronto and then raised six children, although a graduate degree at Oxford was also a possibility; and her Aunt J (Joyce Carmen Barkhouse), who became a well-known writer and mother of two, and with whom Atwood coauthored the children's story *Anna's Pet* in 1980.

Atwood's undergraduate studies in English at Victoria College at the University of Toronto (a college that hired women on faculty, not a university-wide policy at the time) brought her into an atmosphere of intellectual dialogue in which women were, and were expected to be, active participants. Evidence of Atwood's own outspoken involvement can be found in issues of the college literary journal, *Acta Victoriana*, where she wrote poetry and literary criticism under the gender-neutral signature M. E. Atwood and literary spoofs (together with Dennis Lee, later to become one of Canada's best editors, as well as an author of criticism and children's books) under the pen name "Shakesbeat Latweed."

In terms of hardening Atwood's resolve on feminist issues, perhaps equally important as the empowering atmosphere at Victoria College was the antagonism toward women that Atwood was beginning to feel. That Atwood withheld her first name when signing early publications is perhaps the first sign of her perception that there was a certain discrimination against women writers. Certainly, when she began to read her poetry at the Bohemian Embassy (a coffeehouse where some of Canada's best poets honed their craft in competition with the noises of the espresso machine and the washroom, which was positioned right beside the podium), there were far more men than women on the circuit. However, it was here that Atwood met her contemporary Gwendolyn MacEwen, the enthralling young poet whose voice and appearance would captivate the audience. The atmosphere of the Bohemian Embassy is depicted in Atwood's story "Isis in Darkness." Selena is MacEwen: "slight, almost wispy," with "long, dark hair with a centre part," "eyes outlined in black" and a voice that was "darkly spiced, like cinnamon, and too huge to be coming out of such a small person" (*Wilderness Tips* 55). Over the next few years, Atwood and MacEwen would share many conversations about the practical realities of becoming, and surviving as, a female poet in the male-dominated literary world of their time. This was the 1960s after all, the world—as Atwood points out—of *Playboy*, of Jack Kerouac's *On the Road*, of *The Ginger Man* and *The White Goddess* (Sullivan 103). Both young women succeeded in establishing a strong reputation as poets. Atwood published her first chapbook, *Double Persephone,* in 1961, the same year in which she graduated from Victoria College. She and MacEwen got their big break when they were selected, along with two male poets (George Bowering, now Canada's Poet Laureate, and John Newlove), for inclusion in John Robert Colombo's anthology *Poetry 64.*

Ironically, when Atwood arrived at Radcliffe College (a women's college that became part of Harvard University the year after her arrival) she found that it, too, was largely a man's world. Women weren't given entrance to Lamont Library, where the modern poetry and records (of the vinyl variety—it was the 1960s) were housed. In Victorian Humor, a class she took in her first year at Radcliffe, it was the women who served tea and cookies during the class break. As Atwood puts it, "I always felt a little like a sort of wart or wen on the great academic skin" (in Atwood, "Dancing on the Edge" 77).

Instrumental in cementing Atwood's distinctly feminist resolve were her experiences in the workplace in the 1960s, a time when women did not earn the same salaries as their male counterparts and were not expected to keep their jobs after marriage. In 1963, as a young female employee at Canadian Facts Marketing in Toronto, Atwood watched her coworkers bump up against what is now called the glass ceiling. The company structure was similar to that of Seymour Surveys in *The Edible Woman,* which is described, playfully, as an ice cream sandwich, the women employees forming the gooey middle layer. (For a more detailed account, see the "biographical reading" section in this study's chapter on *The Edible Woman.*)

Consequently, by the time of her first full-length publications (*The Circle Game* in 1966 and *The Edible Woman* in 1969), Atwood was acutely aware of the double standards facing women and was prepared to use her writing to expose them. This project of exposure has become a central tenet of all her writing—fiction, nonfiction, and poetry.

NATIONALIST CONCERNS

In part, Atwood's commitment to writing in, about, and on behalf of Canada was ironically prompted by her experiences abroad. While at graduate school in the States, Atwood encountered firsthand how little people knew of Canada and Canadian culture. Consequently, when, newly married to her Harvard colleague James Polk, she returned to Canada to take up a teaching position at Montreal's Sir George Williams University (now Concordia University) in 1967, she was attuned to the importance of fostering a Canadian literary community and committed to being a member of it. That nationalist impulse was in tune with Canada's own mood at the time. Nineteen sixty-seven was the year when Expo was held in Montreal, and Montreal played proud host to the world. It was also the year of Canada's Centennial Celebrations, a time when attention and money were put toward identifying a distinctly Canadian identity.

Despite such a pro-Canada sentiment in the air, in the 1960s, courses and curriculum in university English departments were still largely focused on British and American literature. It wasn't until Atwood returned to Canada in 1970, from a stint of living in Britain, that she first taught a course in Canadian literature at York University in Toronto. Even then, questions posed during Atwood's readings suggested that Canadians knew very little about their own literature. Consequently, when Atwood's old school chum Dennis Lee asked her to join the editorial board of Anansi Press, a small press he had cofounded with Dave Godfrey and one devoted to publishing the work of new Canadian writers as well as works of social value, she agreed. Further, when the editorial board brainstormed ideas about a book that might be popular enough to make some money for the press, an introductory handbook to Canadian literature seemed like just the thing. As a result, Atwood wrote *Survival* to fill a perceived need—both in terms of Canadian literature and Anansi Press. *Survival* quickly became an international best seller. With the list of "suggested readings" compiled by Ann Wall and attached to each chapter, it proved to be an ideal teachers' guide. It also provided a readable discussion of the ways in which the Canadian environment seemed to have shaped the literature of its writers.

Atwood and Polk both became involved with Anansi, taking on a commitment that was more like a lifestyle than a job. Indeed, Polk remained there after Atwood's departure in 1972. Its cofounder, Dennis Lee, and Atwood both compare their commitment to Anansi with giving blood. The heady environment of the 1970s—together with long hours of work, lots of alcohol (Anansi was beside the Red Lion pub on Jarvis Street by then), and a genuine sense of purpose—made for an intensity that could not last. Nevertheless, during these years, Anansi engendered some of the key texts of Canadian literature—*Five Legs* by Graeme Gibson (whom Atwood met at Anansi, and who would become her partner in 1972), Northrop Frye's *The Bush Garden*, Atwood's *Power Politics*, George Grant's *Technology and Empire*, Dennis Lee's *Civil Elegies*, Michael Ondaatje's *Coming through Slaughter*, and George Bowering's *The Gangs of Kosmos*.

It also had its casualties. Atwood and Polk's marriage, already floundering by the time they returned to Canada, disintegrated. Furthermore, Russell Marois, a young writer who lived in the basement at Anansi, committed suicide by lying on the railway tracks near the symbolically named Port Hope. He had no identification on him except for the Anansi phone number. He must have known that Shirley Gibson, with whom he had an affair, would have been the one to answer the phone, although Dennis Lee was ultimately the one who identified the body. Shirley Gibson's collection of poetry, *I Am Watching*, provides additional background to this period in Anansi's history.

Atwood's novel of this time, *Life before Man*, was very well received abroad (Australian-born British critic Coral Ann Howells cites this as the novel that brought Atwood "international recognition" [2]), but it received mixed reviews in Canada. In part, this may have been because it was seen to be a roman à clef, or a rendition of real events thinly disguised as fiction, of the Anansi time. The parallels were not as obvious as those in the roman à clef written by Ellen Godfrey, wife of Anansi founder, Dave Godfrey. In her *The Case of the Cold Murderer*, the similarities between fiction and life were shockingly apparent.

Life before Man also announced Atwood's resolve to write what she calls "autogeography," that is, fiction grounded in absolute geographical accuracy. For example, the place names are not provided in her first novel, *The Edible Woman*, written at a time when Canadians perceived that all-important literature was set in locations outside Canada. By the time Atwood wrote *Surfacing*, the highways of her childhood are described in enough detail for locals to recognize the landmarks. However, with the publication of *Life before Man*, the details of Toronto's streets, its restaurants, museums, and landmark buildings are described explicitly. This, too, is a function of the nationalist impulse behind Atwood's writing.

CONCERNING THE WRITER

Atwood quotes fellow Canadian writer, Alistair MacLeod, as saying "that you write about what worries you" (in Noah Richler 3).

Certainly, the three themes traced here are responses to what worries Atwood: threats to the environment; to women's rights, and to human rights, more generally; as well as to Canadian cultural autonomy. But her writing reveals another deep-seated concern. There is, to put it rather vaguely, a dark strain in Atwood's writing. It is often described as the "gothic" strain of her work—its fascination with ambiguous characterization, eerie settings, and the evocation of terror, to cite the key characteristics of the gothic aesthetic. Atwood's fascination with gothic themes is evident throughout her oeuvre, but especially in *Good Bones* (a collection of short prose pieces), *Murder in the Dark* (a collection of prose poems and short stories), and *Strange Things: The Malevolent North in Canadian Literature* (four lectures about what she calls the "outré menu" aspects of Canadian literature, its monsters and legends [3]). When the literary critic Coral Ann Howells traces the gothic strain in Atwood's work, she focuses largely on the novels: *Lady Oracle, Surfacing,* and *The Robber Bride* (in Howells 62–85). But, at some level, most of Atwood's work is gothic. It certainly contains elements of threat: characters with questionable morals (especially in the villainess novels) or a loose grip on reality (*The Edible Woman, Surfacing, The Journals of Susanna Moodie*); nightmarish settings (in *Bodily Harm,* as well as novels set in a speculative future); ghostly apparitions (*Surfacing, Lady Oracle*); or, perhaps most frightening of all, a bleak vision of our own society's future (in the speculative fictions, *The Handmaid's Tale* and *Oryx and Crake*).

Where does the darkness of Atwood's writing come from? The first and most obvious source of this darkness comes from Atwood's own fascination with things gothic and supernatural, and her recognition that powerful stories involve villains. As a young child, she devoured the unexpurgated version of Grimms' fairy tales, relishing the range of characters and roles. As a teenager, her summer reading included mystery novels, including those of Dashiell Hamett (in Atwood, "On the Trail of Dashiell Hammett" R1, R7). Also, on weekends she could be found in her father's library, which was full of history books and stories of battle. As an undergraduate, she explored the role of the supernatural in the writing of Henry James (later emulating his method in the ghostly projections of *Surfacing* and *Lady Oracle*) and studied John Milton (with the formidable Northrop Frye, then a professor at Victoria College). As a graduate student at Harvard, she began writing a doctoral dissertation on the nineteenth-century metaphysical romance, itself an inheritor of the gothic novel. Put bluntly, Atwood's wide and eclectic reading has frequently taken her to unlit places.

But Atwood's fascination with decidedly dark forms of writing doesn't quite answer the question about why her nonfictional discussions of writing and her fictional depictions of writers involve so much darkness. Quite honestly, I have always dodged this question, because of my firm conviction that a writer has a rare imaginative ability and can therefore, to put it bluntly, make up a good story. Isn't this, after all, the power and magic of a good writer and storyteller? Atwood, too, underlines the element of "artistry," in the difference between "true confessions and writing a novel" (in Atwood, "Witch Craft" 31).

Michael Rubbo, in his 1984 film, *Once in August*, tackles the question head on. He sets out to locate the source of Atwoodian gothic, expecting to find in it some combination of Atwood's childhood and her childhood environment. His film records the ways in which his quest is stymied. Rubbo's mood gets darker. The incessant rain during his stay on the island and his sore back probably didn't help things (Atwood, Letter to the author, 28 November 1995). In the film, Atwood's family seems positively sunny: as Atwood's father surveys his dock; as her daughter Jess bathes in the lake, the sun reflected in her Botticelli curls; as Gibson sings her a song in the cabin's nighttime calm; as Atwood's mother puts the finishing touches on an apple pie, her eyes a twinkle she describes Peggy's younger years. No dysfunctional family this.

What, then, can we make of the dark strain in Atwood's writing? So far, we have lumped together the various strains of darkness in Atwood's writing, either as gothic or, as in this study, as some combination of the gothic (the creation of darkness) and the satiric (the exposure of darkness). In terms of the work itself, combining the two is accurate and justified. However, in terms of teasing out the various sources of those darker elements in her writing, they need to be distinguished more carefully. I'm going to suggest that there are actually four shades of darkness in Atwood's work that translate into the stages in which a central character perceives her (and I'm using the female form of the pronoun since, in Atwood's work, this is the general case) relationship to it. Stage one, threat: when darkness is perceived as a vague threat from outside. Stage two, recognition: when the nature of that darkness is recognized. Stage three, self-recognition: when the darkness is perceived to be within as well as without. Stage four, error: when the quality of darkness becomes ambiguous, as the central character looks more closely at it. In the analytical chapters that follow, the novels' central characters will take this journey toward taking responsibility for their own error or involvement in what they perceive to be darkness. A key insight comes from Marilyn French, who writes:

> For almost thirty years, I have depended on Margaret Atwood for books that treat women as full human beings. It is still rare for writers, female or male, to depict women as intelligent, active beings with the capacity for moral choice and moral error: they are still often depicted as people whose single choice concerns the disposal of their genital organs. I count on Atwood to be brilliant, perceptive, profound and searching, someone who does not avoid the "darker" sides of female being, the weak or wavering or foolish. (in Nischik 310)

When one looks at Atwood's own discussion of her relationship to writing, one can recognize a similar journey through the four shades, or stages, of darkness.

Stage One: Darkness Threatens

The first stage corresponds to that of "threat"—in Atwood's case, her initial impressions about the vocation she had chosen at the age of five or, in her account, which had chosen her on a fateful walk across her high-school football field. Either way, by the time she had declared to the high-school yearbook editor that her ambition was "to write the great Canadian novel," her mind was clearly made up. To put it mildly, the prospects for women artists, especially poets, were pretty bleak. First, as Virginia Woolf had noted in *A Room of One's Own*, there were relatively few of them. Second, as Atwood points out in "The Curse of Eve or What I Learned in School," they were not a healthy and happy bunch: eccentric (George

Eliot, Colette), unmarried (Jane Austen, Emily Dickinson), isolated (Chris-
tina Rossetti), or clinically depressed to the point of being suicidal (Virginia Woolf, Sylvia Plath, Anne Sexton) (*Second Words* 224–25). For
Atwood, the biographies of "Suicidal Sylvia, Reclusive Rossetti and Elu-
sive Emily" were cautionary tales. Sadly, the biographies of some promi-
nent Canadian women writers are not much more positive: witness the
death (at her husband's hand) of poet Pat Lowther and the alcohol ad-
diction and untimely deaths of Gwendolyn MacEwen and Margaret Laurence. Atwood's conclusion: "[I]t *is* more difficult for a woman writer in
this society than for a male writer . . . because it has been made more
difficult . . . the stereotypes still lurk in the wings, ready to spring" (226).

Stage Two: Recognizing the Darkness

That popular portrayals of women artists acknowledged this darkness
must have made it seem all the more threatening. Atwood remembers, in
particular, seeing the Moira Shearer film called *The Red Shoes* at a birthday
party in 1948. Here, a ballerina finds herself forced to make a choice between her dancing and her marriage. She chooses marriage but, after sti-
fling the desire to dance for as long as possible, she decides to put her red
dancing shoes on just for one last time. The film ends as she dances onto
the train tracks, in the path of an oncoming train. The threatening moral
was clear for the young Atwood: you can be either a wife and mother *or*
an artist, but not both. Just how threatening this was for Atwood is clear
from the way the "dancing girl" image reverberates throughout Atwood's
fiction: in the title of a short story collection, *Dancing Girls;* in the damaged
feet (Joan's gashed from glass in *Lady Oracle,* Elaine's damaged from her
habit of picking at them in *Cat's Eye*); in the red shoes (worn, for example,
by Offred and mentioned as she plays Scrabble with the Commander in
The Handmaid's Tale). Recognition, then, the second shade of darkness,
came very early to Atwood. In her generation, she understood that a
woman artist had to make a choice: either her art, and the bleak life that
promised to entail, or a life that involved marriage, children, and the
various comforts of normalcy.

Stage Three: Recognizing the Darkness Within

Arguably, self-recognition, or the third stage, came when Atwood
gleaned that, even though she clearly did want the pleasures of a normal
life, she was and would always be double: woman *and* writer.

The model of individuals as *being* double, of course, first came to Atwood through her early reading. The notion of an alter ego or shadow
self appeared in the comic books, which she and her older brother Harold,
now an expert in the field of neurophysiology, used to read as children.
For every Superman there was a Clark Kent, for every Spiderman a Peter
Parker. When Wonder Woman was kissed, she got a bit weak in the knees.
That sense of being double must have struck Atwood as especially familiar. After all, named "Margaret" after her own mother, she is actually
called "Peggy" by her friends and family. Although Atwood has adopted
a number of different pseudonyms throughout her career (M. E. Atwood
for early serious publications; Charlatan Botchner, as illustrator of her own
book *Up in the Tree*; Bart Gerrard, as cartoonist for a series of strips in *This
Magazine*; and Shakesbeat Latweed, the pen name for her combined efforts
with Dennis Lee, published in the college journal *Acta Victoriana*), that
distinction between Margaret and Peggy has remained consistent. "Margaret" is the writer, the international celebrity, who takes her vocation very
seriously indeed. "Peggy" is the one who manages not to take herself too
seriously.

As well, Atwood began to notice this pattern of the twinned self in the
writers around her long before the publication of her more generalized
comments on the writer's double life (published in *Negotiating with the
Dead*). Dennis Lee, for example, was both the kindly children's author,
responsible for such hits as *Alligator Pie*, and also one of Canada's leading
editors and critics (in Atwood, "Dennis Lee Revisited" 15). In 1975, she
made the observation in relation to Quebec writer Marie-Claire Blais (in
Atwood, "Marie-Claire Blais"). In 1989, she comes back to the issue in
relation to poet George Bowering (in "Bowering Pie" 3–6). What these
observations suggest is that, as for the wizard in Oz, there is a life-size
person at the helm of the machinery of illusion.

The same goes for Atwood herself. In her autobiographical commentary, Atwood describes herself as distinctly life-size. Whereas her Aunt
Kay remembers Atwood, at age five, declaring her intention to be a writer
(Cogswell), Atwood's own version is far less presumptuous. She describes
herself "scuttling" across a football field in high school when the thumb
of writerly fate descended upon her ("Why I Write Poetry" 44). Rather than
describing her career as involving strategic decisions, she describes being
"blown" by the winds of change (Atwood, Letter to the author). Her an-
ecdotes about her younger self are endearingly and self-deprecatingly
funny. Take the "Case of the Crazed Cashier," for example. Here she describes her job as a cashier at the Venture Inn, where she frazzled around

like "a trapped Junebug, shedding hairpins, dripping cloth or filthy plate in hand" while her boss pointed her out to various customers as the employee with an MA from Harvard (46). Another example would be "A Flying Start," an account of the time when a television camera caught a flying squirrel scrabbling inside her dress.

The irony of such self-deprecation and endearment is that it's a very powerful form of engagement. Atwood knows this. In the 1970s, under the pen name Bart Gerrard, Atwood sketched a series of comics about Survivalwoman. She was a tiny kilt-clad superheroine who looked a lot like Atwood. In one episode, Survivalwoman confronts the American "Superham," using deflationary wit rather than brawn as her weapon—and she wins. So, too, when Atwood uses her pen as a weapon, she aims to win. The alter ego of life-size Peggy is the writer, Margaret. This is the Margaret who speaks up on issues of national concern (Free Trade, Quebec Separatism, Bush's invasion of Iraq) and who advocates for other writers (through involvement in the Canadian Writers Union, Amnesty International, PEN Canada, and PEN International). This is the writer who, in *The Handmaid's Tale*, projects the geographical reality of Harvard Yard into the nightmarish future of the Republic of Gilead so as to satirize or "shed light" on some of the darker aspects of our present society: most obviously, the double standards involving gender.

Stage Four: Writing from the Place of Darkness

The fourth and last stage in this process of facing the darkness and recognizing it as something familiar is when one can speak from a place of darkness. This is the moment when Atwood's heroines not only display their "capacity for moral error" (as Marilyn French put it) but also explore the depths of error. The word *error*, one must remember, involves the notion of wandering inherent in the verb *to err*. As such, Atwood's heroines don't "fall" from grace in one sudden dramatic gesture reminiscent of the villain of Milton's *Paradise Lost* or the woman undone in nineteenth-century novels. Instead, they "stray" from the right path or "wander" into the realms of darkness. This study concludes by analyzing *The Blind Assassin*, a novel in which the central character does just this. The novel is narrated by the remarkably sympathetic 80-something Iris Griffen, who has indeed reached a point of moral and ethical darkness.

The darkness from which Atwood speaks is not that of ethical or moral ambiguity. Quite the opposite, her sharp wit prompts her to be very clear about the butts of her satire. Rather, as an artist, Atwood must mine the depths of memory and observation, and then transform the gems she finds into art. That process of transformation, one pursued by each writer alone with the page in front of her, is the writer's darkness.

Perhaps this is best illustrated in the struggle of the artist in *Cat's Eye*, Elaine, to transform through art the memories of her childhood, themselves dark and then kept in the dark because she forgets them for so long. Another example involves the process of writing *Cat's Eye*, a novel that took Atwood about 20 years to write.

It's not unusual for Atwood to begin a novel and then put it aside, in a drawer, only to come back to it later from a new angle. However, this particular one, drawing very closely on the details of her childhood, proved particularly troublesome. It was begun in 1964–1965, the year Atwood spent at the University of British Columbia, when she wrote four short stories: "The Ravine," "Scribblers," "Suffer the Little Children" and "Cut-Out." As they were revised, Judith McCombs explains, these would become the basis for scenes in the novel.

Atwood didn't return to this subject matter until the late 1980s. By this time, her daughter Jess (born in 1976 to Atwood and Gibson) was herself in adolescence, and Atwood must have had the chance to overhear the patterns of speech and habit of a group of young girls. Moreover, two pieces in *Murder in the Dark* (1984) provide evidence that Atwood went back to the material of *Cat's Eye* in the mid-1980s. In one, "Horror Comics," the speaker tells her friend "C" that she is a vampire, in a conversation reminiscent of Elaine's with Cordelia in *Cat's Eye* as she begins to get the upper hand in their relationship. In another sequence of *Murder in the Dark*, "Fainting," the speaker explains how she can "slip sideways" out of time, a discovery that resembles one of Elaine's early means of escaping her childhood tormentor, Cordelia (16).

Atwood began writing a journal in the mid-1980s as well, and sections of that journal bear a striking correspondence to passages in the novel. In the "Ox Eyes" passage, a young girl watches the Santa Claus parade, as Elaine does in the novel, from a Zoology-building window; "Ravines" depicts a descent into a world removed from wakefulness, and a brother who wins elegantly at marbles and hides his winnings deep in the ravine in glass jars (Margaret Atwood Papers, Box 90:22). Whether these journal entries depict real life or are simply sketched in preparation for a longer work is unclear. It is clear, however, that *Cat's Eye* draws heavily on autobiographical material: the neighborhood of Atwood's childhood, the circle of her friends, and her family's neighbors at the time.

I have argued elsewhere that *Cat's Eye* is not pure autobiography but rather provides the illusion of Elaine's autobiography in a writerly equivalent of the magician's deft sleight of hand ("Politics"). It is also true that this novel draws on autobiographical material, largely from Atwood's childhood, and then transforms it into a tightly structured fiction that develops momentum through its use of symbol. The question of how to structure the details of her childhood, how to find a "literary home" for her memories of that time was a dark cloud that hung over the novel's material for 20-odd years.

WRITING AS A DARK ART

These four stages suggest that, for Atwood, writing is a fascinating but dark art—one where shadows lurk, not only in the subject matter (as those who identify the gothic or satiric elements suggest), but also in the author's role as a double being, and in the writing process itself, in which the writer must not only face the darkness, but learn to see in and through it. Atwood, however, is adamant that art itself provides a means of "see[ing] in the dark" (*Cat's Eye* 27). Artist friend Charlie Pachter phrased the question bluntly to the 29-year-old Atwood: "Is it true that artists have to suffer to be creative?" (Atwood, Letter to Charles Pachter). Atwood's response was that her answer to this question had evolved through at least two "stages": first yes, thinking that she "had to," and then no, rationalizing a distinction between "paying a price" and "suffering" (Atwood, Letter to Charles Pachter). The darkness in and of Atwood's writing, I suggest, is the value of that price.

2

Literary Heritage

Atwood's work is located at the intersection of three distinct, though related, literary traditions: feminist, Canadian nationalist, and postmodern. Writers in all three of these traditions share an acute sense of belatedness, of coming *after* all the great stories have been told. Further, they also question the appropriateness of the great stories they have inherited in relation to their own experience in the contemporary moment. As women, as Canadians, as postmodern thinkers, these writers feel very distant in time, place, and perspective from the Avon of Shakespeare, for example, or from the Lake Country of Wordsworth.

Of course, at some level, all writers experience this feeling of belatedness. One of the best-known articulations of literary belatedness appears in "Autumn Refrain," a poem by the American Romantic poet Wallace Stevens. Living in the United States, where there are no nightingales, Stevens laments the impossibility of his using such a powerful and established symbol of beauty in a plausible way. "[T]he name of a bird," he writes, "I have never—shall never hear." While Stevens's poem pays homage to Keats's famous "Ode to a Nightingale," it also refuses to emulate it. Two famous critical treatises also touch on the issue of belatedness. In *The Anxiety of Influence,* Harold Bloom argues that writers are driven by the simultaneous desire to acknowledge and distinguish themselves from their literary forebears. T. S. Eliot in "Tradition and the Individual Talent" further places each new writer or text within a historical continuum, reflecting and refracting (in the same way that a prism reflects and refracts light) those who have gone before. By this, Eliot means that writers can and must extend the Tradition, but that they can only do so by coming to know and appreciate it. Here, "Tradition" implies a canon, or selection of works that includes the best work of the best writers.

One paradox is that writers who experience an acute sense of belatedness have a deep respect for and fascination with the great stories, yet at the same time they seek to undermine them because of their search for new stories and new ways of telling stories. Atwood is no exception. Peculiar to Atwood, though, is the extent to which she has articulated her own sense of belatedness in her nonfiction. Indeed, this is one theme that links the six Empson lectures (the most dominant theme being an exploration of writing and its motivations), first delivered at the University of Cambridge and later published as *Negotiating with the Dead* in 2002.

There are three epigraphs to *Negotiating with the Dead:* to the Brothers Grimm, Geoffrey Chaucer, and Canadian poet A. M. Klein. These epigraphs indicate debts Atwood acknowledges to three broad traditions: fairy tale, and the canons of British and of Canadian literature. The order of their mention corresponds with Atwood's own formation as a writer. She first encountered the fairy tales of the Brothers Grimm, for instance, as a child. Reading the uncensored version with its villains and heroes, Atwood gleaned a lifelong appreciation for the powerful potential of a full range of character types. The most obvious recognition of her debt to fairy tale appears in works that speak directly to "The Robber Bridegroom," including her novel *The Robber Bride,* short-story collection *Bluebeard's Egg,* and poems such as "The Robber Bridegroom" and "No Name," collected in *Interlunar.* However, allusions to fairy tale permeate all of her œuvre. Those wishing to pursue this line of inquiry should begin by looking at Sharon Rose Wilson's *Margaret Atwood's Fairy-Tale Sexual Politics,* which provides a thorough and comprehensive close analysis of the fairy-tale contexts of Atwood's work through 1992.

The second epigraph of *Negotiating with the Dead,* taken from Geoffrey Chaucer's masterpiece of the Middle Ages, *The Canterbury Tales* (late fourteenth century), is prompted by Atwood's respect for the British literary tradition. As an undergraduate university student at the University of Toronto's Victoria College, Atwood followed a rigorous program of study in English literature. It was organized chronologically, both to give students access to the great works of the Tradition and to familiarize them with the context of those works. Atwood remembers her years at the University of Toronto with fondness (Cooke, *Margaret Atwood* 57–58).

Significantly, the well-respected critic Northrop Frye was teaching at Victoria College when Atwood was there. It was from Frye himself, considered the contemporary authority on the subject, that Atwood studied the Bible. Frye's insistence on the Bible's role as *the* foundational text of the Western tradition can be traced in the writing of his pupils. For example, we can detect Frye's influence in arguments about the pervasiveness of Old Testament figures such as the Leviathan in studies of Canadian literature written by Doug Jones *(Butterfly on Rock)* and Margaret Atwood. Most obviously, however, we can see evidence for his argument in most of Atwood's novels. Even the futuristic novel *The Handmaid's Tale* describes a society whose tenets are drawn directly from the Old Testament.

In her graduate studies in English at Radcliffe College, Atwood worked under the supervision of another authority on the British literary tradition, Jerome Buckley. At the time she was at Radcliffe, Buckley was working on *Season of Youth: The Bildungsroman from Dickens to Golding,* his study of bildungsroman, or novels that describe the development from youth to maturity of a fictional character. The subgenre of the bildungsroman is the *künstlerroman* ("artist novel"), which depicts the formation of an artist, the paradigm or acknowledged example of which is James Joyce's *Portrait of the Artist as a Young Man.* This novel documents Stephen Dedalus's (his last name is an allusion to the myth of Icarus and his artist-inventor father, Dedalus) development and emergence as a writer in twentieth-century Ireland. Other examples of the form that are identified by Buckley include *Great Expectations, Sons and Lovers,* and *Jude the Obscure* (viii). Atwood's own *künstlerroman* is *Cat's Eye,* a novel that engages this form explicitly while also recasting the protagonist as a woman. However, one of the recurring figures in all her writing is that of the artist. Did Atwood glean an appreciation for the potential of this figure while listening to Buckley's lectures at Radcliffe College?

An important Canadian recontextualization of the *künstlerroman* is a poem (rather than a *roman,* the French word for novel) written by A. M. Klein entitled "Portrait of the Poet as Landscape." Atwood uses a section of this poem as the third and last epigraph for *Negotiating with the Dead.* As such, it not only serves to indicate her engagement with literary portraits of the artist, a tradition discussed above, but also her acknowledgment of the Canadian literary tradition (the influence of which will be discussed later in the chapter). The particular section she chooses tells of a poet who "climbed / another planet" in his imagination so as to get a heightened perspective "upon this earth," a perspective that he would later use for his work. In other words, this passage emphasizes the writer's dual responsibility to witness and document the world, all the time taking full advantage of the writerly imagination. This imperative of witness is evident throughout Atwood's work, tending at times toward satire, a form of writing that exaggerates in order to expose, and thereby correct, particular aspects of contemporary society. As a satirist, Atwood follows a long tradition whose path is marked by such literary milestones as Jonathan Swift's *Gulliver's Travels* and George Orwell's *Animal Farm*. In Canada, the satiric tradition has included the humorous irony of Stephen Leacock *(Sunshine Sketches of a Little Town)* and the biting wit of Mordecai Richler (whose novels include *The Apprenticeship of Duddy Kravitz* and the Booker Award–winning *St. Urbain's Horseman*). Atwood has collected a number of Canadian works in the satiric tradition in a collection entitled *Barbed Lyres*. The collection's title puns on the satiric artist's way of using his instrument for the particular purpose of poking fun at the object of his satire. The lyre is usually associated with the gentle music this harp-like instrument can produce, and it was the instrument used to accompany the recital of poetry in its earlier days in Greece. Consequently, *"barbed" lyres* suggests a music that is far less gentle.

In addition to acknowledging debts to literary traditions, Atwood's fiction and poetry engage with the cultural context of her day, most often to question the assumptions behind various conventions. For example, "Miss July Grows Older," a poem from *Morning in the Burned House* (21), takes aim at the conventions of calendars produced by magazines such as *Playboy*. Spoken by Miss July herself, now an older woman, the poem gives voice to the figure conventionally portrayed as silent. References to popular culture in Atwood's work are motivated by two imperatives. The first is what Atwood calls an "autogeographical" impulse, her desire to depict a particular moment and place in time as accurately as possible. In fact, she researches the settings of her novels very carefully, checking that particular items in the landscape were really there at the time in which her novels are set. Part of describing a particular moment in time, of course, involves describing what people wear, eat, use, buy, and say. The second impulse behind Atwood's incorporation of references to popular culture in her work is her desire to link contemporary concerns, as exemplified in the popular culture of the day, to those addressed by the great literary masters. *Lady Oracle*, for example, asks its reader to interpret its main character within the context of fairy tale, Disney films, "costume gothic romances" (of the Harlequin dime-story variety), and the tradition of Courtly Love.

ATWOOD AND THE TRADITION OF ANGLO-AMERICAN FEMINISM

Through mixing such references to "high" and "low" art, or intellectual and popular traditions, Atwood's work both overturns the tradition of distinguishing between high and low art and aligns itself with the post-modern impulse to challenge established conventions. However, the particular literary conventions at which Atwood's work most often takes aim tend to be those relegating women to the sidelines of the story, casting them in secondary and passive roles. As a consequence, Atwood's work can fruitfully be described as feminist, and useful comparisons can be drawn between her writing and that of other feminist writers in the twentieth century.

Moreover, the particular ways in which her work rewrites literary convention situates it squarely in the Anglo-American tradition of feminist writing. That phrase, *Anglo-American,* draws attention to its dual British and American heritage, but also distinguishes it from the other significant line of feminist inquiry—French. The principal focus of French feminists, including Hélène Cixous, Toril Moi, Luce Irigaray, and Julia Kristeva, is to challenge the conventions of language. Anglo-American feminists, by contrast, tend to challenge the conventions of plot and characterization. Of course, as with any such general distinction, there are exceptions. American writers Gertrude Stein and H. D. (Hilda Dolittle), for example, are known for their experimentation with language use. However, Anglo-American feminism is well illustrated through the work of its foundational practitioners: Virginia Woolf in Britain, Kate Chopin in America, and Doris Lessing in South Africa.

Anthologies surveying the tradition of women's writing include examples of work written by women, some of which could accurately be described as feminist even though the term had not come into existence before the twentieth century. Two important critical studies identify the conventions associated with women's roles in the novelistic tradition. In *The Mad Woman in the Attic,* Sandra Gilbert and Susan Gubar argue that the nineteenth-century novel offered limited plot alternatives to its female characters, either marriage on the one hand or death or madness on the other. What distinguishes twentieth-century women's fiction from that of the nineteenth-century, according to Rachel Blau DuPlessis, is the way in which novelists write "beyond the ending." In other words, they allow their characters to pursue other alternative trajectories and examine what happens after marriage or, as in Atwood's *Lady Oracle* and the poem "This is a Photograph of Me" (from *The Circle Game*), after death. Atwood's fiction also allows women to play roles usually reserved for men. In *The Robber Bride*, for example, the Robber Bridegroom of the Grimms' fairy tale is recast as a bride. One of the implications of such feminist revisions to plot is that the story lines that drive Atwood's fiction are not romances. Rather, with the exception of *Oryx and Crake*, which centers on a male protagonist, Atwood's novels rehearse a range of different ways in which women come, with varying degrees of success, to voice and power. Interestingly, *Life before Man* traces that same journey in relation to at least three different characters—two women and one man.

Although Atwood's work is known for its feminist critique of the Tradition, it has also gained canonical status to the extent that it has now become part of that Tradition. Consequently her own work has itself become a subject for writerly revision. Marian Engel's 1976 novel *Bear*, for instance, engages in a dialogue with Atwood's novel *Surfacing*. Most interesting from a feminist point of view are some recent works by Canadian writers that expose Atwood's feminism as distinctly white, middle class, and centrist (meaning aligned with dominant lines of thought). The most vehement and recent comment in this vein comes from Stephen Henighan in *When Words Deny the World*.

ATWOOD AND THE CANADIAN LITERARY TRADITION

A resident for part of the year in Toronto, Atwood is a Canadian writer, and one who has been instrumental in the development of Canadian literary practice and of Canadian literature as a discipline of scholarly study. Analyses of her work can be significantly enriched by attention to the Canadian literary and cultural context. Readers of *Alias Grace* who are unfamiliar with the trial of Paul Bernardo will miss an illustration of the same gender dynamics at play in the last decade of the twentieth century that are described in Atwood's historical novel. Indeed, news of the Bernardo trial coincided with the novel's release in bookstores across Canada. After all, while Paul Bernardo was condemned for his crime, his wife, like Grace in the novel, received a lesser sentence. Similarly, readers unfamiliar with the history of Anansi Press in the 1970s, including the tragic suicide of writer Russell Marois and the various relationships between those on the editorial board of the press, would miss one way of reading *Life before Man*.

Canadian literature until the 1970s was characterized, according to Atwood's seminal critical study, *Survival,* by the theme of a struggle for survival. In *Survival,* Atwood identifies a trajectory of different victim positions and then divides Canadian literary works into groups according to the victim position they articulate. Critic George Woodcock argues that Atwood's own novel, *Surfacing,* is an illustration of victim position number four, which involves being a "creative non-victim" (53). (Indeed, Woodcock finds that all Atwood's heroines belong in this category.) A number of other critics, including Joan Harcourt, Val Clery, and Bonnie Lyons, trace the striking similarities between *Survival* and *Surfacing.*

The sheer popularity of Atwood's *Survival,* which served as a primer for teachers as well as students, had a profound influence on the way Canadians perceived their own literary tradition. Its appearance, together with the founding of the Canada Council granting agency in 1957 and the development in 1958 of McClelland and Stewart's New Canadian Library paperback series of key Canadian novels, alerted Canadians to the fact that they indeed had a literary tradition. By 1978, the date of an important literary conference in Calgary, Canadian literature had become a subject of study at the university level. Robert Lecker asserts that Canadian literature appeared in schools toward the end of the Second World War (25). William H. New locates its entrance into the schools shortly thereafter, in 1960 (213). Atwood herself taught a course on Canadian literature at York University in the early 1970s. Consequently, Atwood emerged on the Canadian literary scene just as Canadian literature itself became institutionalized and made its entrance onto the world stage. Atwood, as Coral Ann Howells puts it, has "made Canadians known to themselves and the international community. For an international readership her project has been that of 'translating Canada', mapping its geography, its history of European exploration and settlement, its literary and artistic heritage and its cultural myths" (10).

Canadian literature, of course, has a much longer history. Frances Brooke's novel, *The History of Emily Montague* (1769), is often said to be the first work of Canadian literature, and different commentators argue about the significance of other milestones in the development of this relatively new (by British and American standards) literary canon. Was Gabrielle Roy's *Bonheur d'occasion* (later translated and published under the title *The Tin Flute*) the first Canadian novel of urban realism that paved the way for such acclaimed "city novels" as the Toronto novels of Ondaatje (*In the Skin of a Lion*) and Atwood (*Life before Man, Cat's Eye,* and *The Robber*

Bride, to name just three)? Was Gwethalyn Graham's *Swiss Sonata* Canada's first international best seller that broke the path for such Booker Prize–winning novelists as Mordecai Richler, Margaret Atwood, and Rohinton Mistry? Was Alice Munro's story collection *Lives of Girls and Women* the first to scrutinize everyday experience from a specifically female perspective, and did it set a precedent for the candid first-person narrations of such later writers as Margaret Atwood and of such powerful voices as Morag Gunn's in Margaret Laurence's *The Diviners?*

What are the works of Canadian literature that have most influenced Atwood? One answer involves looking at the canon, or group of "serious" texts recognized as a central body of works, that she assembles in *Survival.* By identifying writing that has shaped Canadian literature, Atwood points to the Canadians whose works she herself has read closely and which have, in many cases, shaped her own thinking. Among the writers mentioned in *Survival,* a few stand out as having influenced her work in significant ways. Atwood's very first collection of poetry, *Double Persephone* (1961), owes much to the influence of poet Jay Macpherson, who was also her instructor at Victoria College. Atwood's survival thesis itself develops the arguments of another one of her professors at Victoria College: Northrop Frye. It was Frye who identified a garrison mentality (the desire to take refuge against the onslaught of the wilderness or the unknown) in Canadian literature. Atwood identifies it as one stage in the struggle for survival.

Atwood does not mention her own novels in *Survival,* although two of her poetry collections, *The Journals of Susanna Moodie* and *The Animals in That Country* do appear on the "long list" of selected readings, compiled by Ann Wall. But she does discuss the work of her contemporaries in a way that contextualizes her own practice. It is hard not to see the works of Margaret Laurence, Alice Munro, and Margaret Atwood as engaging in a discussion about the function of the female artist figure in their day. In subsequent years, this novelistic discussion will expand to include works by other Canadian women writers, including Carol Shields, Audrey Thomas, and Susan Swan.

Atwood is best known both outside and within Canada for her fiction, and specifically her novels. Her poetry, however, has influenced younger generations of poets in Canada. Lorna Crozier's experiments with rewriting inherited myths from a female point of view owe much to Atwood's feminist revisionism. Stephanie Bolster's exploration of Alice Liddell (Hargreaves), the inspiration for Lewis Carroll's Alice books, pursues the method established by Atwood's *The Journals of Susanna Moodie* for exploring a particular character in poetry from a variety of different perspectives.

ATWOOD AND THE POSTMODERN LITERARY TRADITION

While the challenges posed by Atwood's work are prompted by feminist impulses, the urge to challenge is itself postmodern in nature. Indeed, in such varied realms as literature, art, and architecture, the urge to challenge and to disturb overly rigid categories of classification is one of two key characteristics of postmodernism. The second characteristic is a sense of intellectual playfulness. Both of these characteristics are also evidence of postmodernism's larger objective of exploring the way meaning is created or, to use a theatrical metaphor, of looking beyond the puppet to the hands of the puppeteer and the strings she or he manipulates. In the case of postmodern literary texts, these characteristics often translate into a refusal to supply only one plot and one ending. Instead, postmodern literary texts often resist closure by offering multiple plots and alternative endings. In this way, postmodernists not only tell a story, they also tell the story of how stories are told and understood.

Another way to look at these contemporary Canadian women's challenges to literary conventions, then, is to see them as part of the larger movement of postmodernism in the twentieth century. Canadian critic Linda Hutcheon, in her study *The Canadian Postmodern*, examines the postmodern aspect of a number of Canadian texts of the last decades of the twentieth century. Ultimately, Hutcheon sees a number of these texts (especially those by Margaret Laurence and Sheila Watson's *The Double Hook*) as more modernist than postmodernist, privileging resolution over challenge, closure over disclosure. American critic Molly Hite, however, qualifies Hutcheon's conclusion and contributes to the discussion in ways that clarify the nature of Atwood's postmodernism. Hite argues that postmodern fiction by women *looks* different from postmodern fiction by men. Certainly, key commentators on postmodernism, such as Jean Lyotard (who sees it as signaling the irrelevance of the central stories of Western civilization for contemporary times) and Jean Baudrillard (who sees it as a function of a media-saturated age that has taken us into a new chapter of history), do focus on the radical experimentation of *male* postmodern writers. These include John Barth, whose stories, such as "Lost in the Funhouse," are marked by narrators who interrupt their own stories, and Robert Pynchon, whose *Gravity's Rainbow* frustrates any reader expecting a clear plot or well-developed and consistent characterization. Hite uses

Atwood's *Lady Oracle* to illustrate how this novel offers a satisfyingly good read and, simultaneously, invites readers to question their assumptions about reading. One of the ways it can achieve this simultaneously is through its metafictional nature, as a novel about novel writing and reading. As Patricia Waugh explains in her book *Metafiction,* when a novel describes another novel, it expands the range of possibility for the reader and undermines the single authority of any one story or conclusion.

It is important to remember that postmodernism was imported to Canada, prompted by examples of postmodern practice in the United States by writers like Barth and Pynchon, and translations of theory from France. Key texts here include Ferdinand de Saussure's *Cours de Linguistique Générale* (a collection of essays dealing with the science of language as social convention—generally described as semiotics) and books by Jacques Derrida outlining the slipperiness of the relationship between meaning and word—generally described as "deconstruction." Postmodernism's most visible practitioner in Canada is Robert Kroetsch. In an extended discussion recorded in *Labyrinths of Voice,* Kroetsch proves himself to be an articulate spokesman for the postmodernism spirit of challenge in Canada. His own novel *Badlands* offers its reader a standard story of an explorer's quest or search for dinosaur bones and challenges to that quest story, which are articulated by the explorer's daughter. As an unwriting of quest, it can be fruitfully compared to Atwood's *Surfacing.* Whereas *Badlands's* female narrator repeatedly draws the reader's attention to her critique of her father's quest narrative, however, Atwood's reader is forced to search for reasons why the narrator refuses to leave the island after the mystery has been solved. The challenges of Kroetch's novel are more in keeping with the tradition of male postmodernism as it comes to Canada from its practitioners in the States.

With the exception of Kroetsch's work, however, postmodernism in Canada is different from that practiced abroad and, particularly, in the United States. Proving this statement, however, is tricky, since the range of postmodernisms in Canada by the end of the century cannot be lumped together in one clear category. For example, women writing in French Canada aligned themselves more closely with French feminist practices, particularly with their challenges to the structures of language, and, therefore, tended to publish works that were more overtly experimental in nature. Some English-Canadian writers, including Daphne Marlatt and Gail Scott, aligned themselves with their counterparts in French Canada and, consequently, produced work that challenged the structures of language and read quite differently from the challenges to plot and characterization emerging from novels by Atwood and other English-Canadian writers, notably Carol Shields, Aritha Van Herk, and Alice Munro.

That Atwood does challenge the rules and conventions of writing, and of society more generally, is clear. These challenges, from her earliest published works, are grounded in feminist and nationalist concerns. The next three chapters will trace three different impulses driving Atwood's fiction (feminist, nationalist, and postmodern) and their corresponding themes (women, Canada and the preservation of its wilderness, and writing). These chapters focus on three of Atwood's early novels—chapter three on *The Edible Woman*, chapter four on *Surfacing*, and chapter five on *Lady Oracle*—both because they are strong illustrations of the three central themes and because, as early novels, they introduce some of the characters and concepts that are developed in Atwood's later novels and are therefore crucial to a reader's understanding of Atwood's larger project. *Lady Oracle*, in particular, introduces all three of the literary strategies explored separately and with reference to a representative novel in the three subsequent chapters: namely, rewriting character (chapter six: *Cat's Eye*), setting (chapter seven: *The Handmaid's Tale)*, and plot (chapter eight: *Blind Assassin*). In order to reveal society's privileging of men and male experience, in the artist novels (*Surfacing, Lady Oracle,* and *Cat's Eye*) Atwood casts the women as narrators of the love stories, rather than as the romantic heroines in them, and disrupts traditional notion of closure. Next, in the villainess novels (*The Robber Bride, Alias Grace,* and *Blind Assassin*), she assigns them lead rather than supporting roles and gives them a chance to play roles usually assigned to men—like the role of the villain. So as to expose the inequities of our own society, in the dystopian novels, she restages the story as a nightmarishly exaggerated version of our own society set in either a distant region (*Bodily Harm*) or a mythic future (*The Handmaid's Tale* and *Oryx and Crake*). In her most recent and already bestselling novel, *Oryx and Crake*, Atwood combines these challenges in a way that transforms her postmodern vision, with its desire to challenge, into a classically satiric vision, with its desire to disturb in order to provoke change. Atwood's gift is that at the same time that her work challenges and disturbs, it also entertains. As its author, then, she is both literary celebrity and moral conscience.

3

The Edible Woman (1969)

The Edible Woman, Atwood's first published novel, provides a critique of North American consumer society in the 1960s from a woman's, and more specifically from a feminist, point of view. A social satire, it aims to reveal and thereby correct society's imperfections. As a *feminist* social satire, it takes particular aim at the way society has institutionalized methods of marginalizing and disempowering women. Since it uses exaggeration to expose some of the worst elements of consumer society, it can be both extremely funny and bitingly satiric at the same time. As such, it provides an early glimpse of the wit characteristic of Atwood's writing style and announces a theme that will be a central concern in all her later work: feminism.

PLOT DEVELOPMENT

The "edible woman" of the novel's title is, most obviously, a doll-shaped cake cooked and consumed in the novel's conclusion. However, the title also refers to the novel's main character, Marian MacAlpin, who is so preoccupied with food that she interprets life around her in terms of food consumption, eventually comes to identify with food, and develops a serious eating disorder. Atwood's title directs us to focus less on the events of the novel—punctuated by such romantic milestones as a love affair, a subsequently broken marital engagement, as well as a planned pregnancy and a birth—than on Marian's own interpretation of those events and her response to them.

The novel's three parts tell the story of Marian MacAlpin's relationship to Peter and counterpoint it with descriptions of other romantic relationships in her immediate circle of friends. The first section, comprising chapters 1 through 12, traces her relationship to Peter, culminating in their engagement to marry. The second part, chapters 13 through 30, outlines Marian's growing discomfort with the prospect of marrying Peter and, simultaneously, her body's increasing discomfort with food. The third part, chapter 31, provides a resolution to both these dilemmas as Marian cooks, serves, and eats the doll-shaped cake of the novel's title. Precisely what kind of resolution this cake provides has been the source of much critical debate.

The novel's opening scene, breakfast at the apartment shared by Marian MacAlpin and her roommate Ainsley, serves to establish a specific setting for the story and to introduce the main character and her central concerns, which are food, friends, and surviving daily life with a roommate and nosy landlady. In terms of setting, Atwood is always careful to depict geographical location with great accuracy, and we see this even in such an early novel as *The Edible Woman*. The events take place in Toronto, and we watch Marian move between the residential neighborhoods of the city. However, the city is never named, and the place names are thinly disguised. The novel's "Rosevale," for example, closely resembles the name for Toronto's posh "Rosedale" district. In part, Atwood's reticence to name the location stems from a young writer's hesitation about whether Toronto, in the 1960s when this book was written, ranked with such established literary cities as Paris, London, or Dublin, the setting of James Joyce's masterpieces. Another reason Atwood downplayed the details of geographical location is that the importance of setting in this novel has more to do with *when* the events take place than with *where* they take place. The story is set in the 1960s and depicts the alternatives available for young middle-class women just embarking on a career and considering the possibilities of marriage.

In the first chapter, we witness breakfast conversation through Marian's point of view. Marian, self-described, appears to be the more normal and "sensible" of the two roommates, who are acquaintances rather than close friends. We are introduced to her roommate Ainsley, who greets the morning with a hangover from a party the night before and later asks Marian to pay an equal share of the bill for a bottle of scotch, though Marian knows that Ainsley will drink most of it. (In chapter 14, we find out that Marian is correct in this assumption.) Marian provides many details about food and drinks in this first chapter, thereby alerting the reader to their symbolic importance in the novel as a whole. We learn, for example, that Marian only eats a bowl of cereal and milk for breakfast, rather than the egg she intended. This is the first example of Marian's foregoing food items. Such details catch our attention because Marian opens the chapter by suggesting that something has happened since Friday, when she got up feeling fine. As readers, then, we start to search for clues about what might have gone wrong since Friday, and why.

The first two chapters also establish setting or context by introducing other characters, women who serve as character foils, or characters with whom the central character can be contrasted. The landlady is the first of these character foils. Marian meets her as she rushes to the bus, already late for work because of her breakfast conversation with Ainsley. The landlady is a strict, nosy, middle-aged woman who is raising a girl on her own, for whose sake she wants Marian and Ainsley to act as responsible role models. The landlady confronts Marian about a fire she believes to have occurred the previous evening, and Marian insists it was just pork chops cooking. Nevertheless, Marian misses her bus and ends up catching the next one with Ainsley, who, upon hearing about the landlady's complaint, resents being so heavily supervised.

The other character foils are introduced to us when Marian reaches her office at Seymour Surveys. The stark contrast between Marian's three co-workers, whom she calls the "office virgins," and Ainsley is made clear during the coffee break conversation. Ainsley's exciting job, which requires that she testify at a trial where a man has tried to commit murder with his electric toothbrush, is juxtaposed with dull, dreary life at Seymour Surveys, where the cancellation of a Quebec laxative study is the hottest news. Marian contemplates the bleak prospects for her future at Seymour Surveys, where there seems to be no possibility of promotion. Marian imagines the company in terms of an ice cream sandwich, where powerful and authoritative men occupy the top layer, questionnaire people like herself occupy the gooey middle layer, and low-paid housewives occupy the lowest layer as interviewers, counters, and sorters.

Marriage, as one alternative strategy for advancement, is introduced in chapter 3. However, at this stage of the novel, marriage seems to offer equally bleak prospects. Peter, Marian's boyfriend, is quite depressed to find out that his last bachelor friend, Trigger, is getting married. Peter cancels dinner with Marian, and she ends up taking Ainsley to dinner at her friend Clara's place. The dinner scene at Clara's, described in chapter 4, makes very explicit the realities of married life with children. Clara is pregnant with an unplanned third child, and the household is in complete disarray. The children misbehave. Arthur, the oldest, has two bathroom accidents. Joe, Clara's philosophy-professor husband who takes care of most household chores, cooks a rather disappointing meal. Marian ponders how Clara went from an ideal feminine figure to an exhausted and disgruntled housewife.

Ainsley's intention to conceive a child and raise it without a husband, a strategy she announces in chapter 5, emerges as one possible alternative to the disappointing model of marriage and motherhood offered by Clara and Joe. Marian is against Ainsley's plan and struggles to defend her position against Ainsley's rather convincing arguments. Consequently, when Marian invites her unmarried friend Len Slank to join her and Peter for dinner, she pointedly does not include Ainsley. Besides, Len is known to like young girls, and Ainsley would be too old for his taste. Ainsley, however, needs a father to conceive her child, and she thinks Len Slank would be a good candidate.

In chapter 6, our attention shifts to a series of interviews Marian has agreed to conduct about customer response to Moose Beer, a product aimed specifically at men. Marian interviews three men. The first is a religious man who preaches temperance; the second makes a pass at her; and the third is an unusual young man whom Marian finds difficult to categorize. This third man, Duncan, will fascinate Marian throughout the novel. Similarly, he will always evade her conclusions about him. In this chapter, she thinks at first that he is 15, although he is really 26. In response to her survey, Duncan claims to drink 7 to 10 beers weekly, then claims not to drink it at all, after which it is subsequently revealed that he indeed does drink it when he accepts one offered by his roommate.

If Duncan is hard to categorize, Marian's boyfriend, Peter, can be very easily categorized. He is a young professional with rising expectations. Now in his articling year (a qualifying year in which law students work for a law firm to gain experience before taking the bar examination), Peter lives in a yet-to-be-completed high-rise apartment complex. Marian, too, behaves like an aspiring middle-class wife. Although she does not live with Peter, she performs the duties of the housewife. Marian picks up some groceries on the way to Peter's apartment and mixes him a drink when she arrives. Peter responds by leading her into the bathtub to make love. Although this behavior is slightly unusual, Marian does tell us that they have made love in unusual places before, each time after one of his bachelor friends marries. Marian concludes the lovemaking by turning on the cold-water tap, foreshadowing her eventual reluctance in the relationship.

The two meet Len for a drink later that evening at the Plaza Hotel. Although uninvited, Ainsley appears, dressed in a way that makes her look much younger than her real age so as to better attract Len. Meanwhile, Peter and Len strike up a graphic conversation about rabbit hunting. Marian feels queasy and ends up weeping in the bathroom. Although she rejoins the group after a time, feeling much calmer, she seems to become destabilized later in the evening when she runs away from Peter as the four leave the Plaza Hotel to go to Len's place.

In chapter 9, a rather dramatic chase ensues as Len pursues Marian on foot and Peter follows her in his car. When she is finally cornered, she is unable to explain what motivated her actions. The reader traces the source of her concerns to the earlier discussion about the rabbit chase and specifically to her identification with the rabbit. This suspicion is confirmed when Marian later burrows between Len's couch and the wall. However, another source of anxiety for Marian is revealed when she turns her thoughts to her four-month relationship with Peter. She realizes that things are getting serious and she needs to make a decision. However, an argument quickly erupts between them, and she begins to set out on foot alone. Peter turns up in his car, scolds her for her behavior, and then proposes. At that moment, lightning strikes, providing a clear example of pathetic fallacy, when the external environment mirrors the characters' emotions.

The breakfast scene in chapter 10, one-third of the way through the novel, is perhaps reminiscent of the opening scene. This time, however, Marian rather than Ainsley has the hangover. She announces to Ainsley her engagement, and Ainsley suggests that she marry in the States, where obtaining a divorce is easier. Ainsley herself is hunched over a calendar, where she is planning her "attack" on Len, whom she has selected as the prime candidate to father her child. Peter later joins them for coffee. Conversation seems a bit awkward between them. Is it because they are now engaged? Or perhaps it is because of Marian's subconscious reluctance, signaled by her request that Peter make the decision about when the wedding should take place.

Marian's ambivalence about Peter is contrasted in the next chapter with her fascination with the ambiguous young Duncan. She meets Duncan at the Laundromat and, while waiting for the laundry, they talk about Duncan's roommates, Fish and Trevor, both English graduate students. Marian finds Duncan difficult to read, but she is clearly intrigued with him. They kiss upon parting.

However, this interlude does not seem to affect Marian's decision to marry Peter. In chapter 12, the last chapter of part 1, Marian cements her resolve to settle down and act responsibly, and convinces herself that she and Peter need not end up like Clara and Joe. She decides not to tell her coworkers at the office about the engagement, since she needs to retain her salary until Peter becomes a full-fledged lawyer. Since Marian is a young woman, an engagement announcement would not only signal her intention to marry, but also the possibility of an eventual pregnancy—something Mrs. Bogue, the supervisor, perceives as an "act of disloyalty to the company"(24). She resolves to sort through her things, getting rid of old clothes, books, and two dolls in preparation for the next stage of her life.

In part 2, some cracks begin to appear in Marian's resolve. Marian notices some differences in her behavior but is not able to interpret them. The reader quickly realizes that Marian is feeling threatened by Peter and the impending marriage. For example, while Marian tells herself that she is comfortable with her decision to marry Peter, her body sends her clear signals that it is not so comfortable with her decision. Over lunch, the "office virgins" congratulate Marian on the engagement and, perhaps slightly envious, ask her how she "snagged" Peter. Indeed, they themselves seem to be trying to "snag" a man. After all, Lucy's choice of an unusually upscale restaurant for lunch is part of a plot to "catch" a husband. The whole game strikes Marian, literally, as being rather distasteful. Marian feels her appetite disappear. Although she was starving before lunch, she finds she can eat only a cheese sandwich. Rather than feeling that she has "snagged" Peter, does Marian feel that she herself has been snagged? Tellingly, when the office manager, Mrs. Bogue, explains that the "Underwear Man" (a man who, posing as a Seymour Surveys employee, makes obscene phone calls to women) has struck again, Marian contemplates whether this mystery man is a victim of society or Peter in disguise.

Chapter 14 exposes the threatening elements in a variety of relationships around Marian. Rather than honesty, Marian sees relationships based on ambiguity and deception. When Peter cancels their dinner plans, Marian goes alone to a movie in order to give Ainsley the apartment so that she can seduce Len. In the dark theater, she hears a cracking noise, and when she turns around to investigate, she spots Duncan. She feels the urge to grab his hand but suppresses this desire. Upon returning to the apartment, she is greeted by a distraught landlady who is clad in curlers. She is upset because the man who entered their apartment earlier has not yet come downstairs. Marian reassures her, although she wonders how they are going to sneak Len out in the morning. Entering the apartment, Marian notices that the bottle of scotch she half paid for is almost empty and that the necktie is hanging around the doorknob of her bedroom, the signal that this is where Ainsley chose to make her conquest. Marian has to sleep in Ainsley's messy room.

Marian visits Clara and her new baby in the hospital in chapter 15. While Marian feels that Clara is no longer the "vegetable" she seemed to be during the first fateful dinner party, the baby is described as a "shriveled prune." Clara describes the progress of her son Arthur's toilet training. Although he is now trained, he still hoards his stool and hides it in various locations throughout their home. Marian does not bother to look at the baby and leaves the hospital with a great feeling of escape. Instead of going to dinner with Peter, Marian agrees to go to Duncan's place. He had phoned her earlier in the day to ask her to bring him some wrinkled clothes, to feed his compulsive need to iron. Marian seems confused when she enters Duncan's building. She gets off the elevator at the wrong floor.

What follows in chapter 16 is a rather curious scene of seduction. Duncan explains his compulsion to iron as the need to do something simple and straightforward, as opposed to such other activities as writing complex term papers. He convinces Marian to give him her shirt to iron. She does. Afterwards, while they lie together on the bed, Duncan caressing the robe he had lent her, Marian realizes how self-absorbed Duncan is. As the chapter ends, Duncan's roommates return, and Marian wonders what Duncan is a substitute for—a question to which Duncan replies, "I'm the universal substitute" (160).

Chapter 17 involves a pivotal dinner scene in which Marian seems to become much more conscious about the nature of her anxiety and confronts the reality of her eating disorder. If, over drinks at the Plaza Hotel, Peter's discussion about chasing rabbits unnerved Marian, then, over rare steak at this dinner, Marian becomes decidedly uncomfortable. The meal begins with Peter and Marian's discussion of parenting techniques. Marian advocates understanding, whereas Peter supports physical discipline. When their rare steaks arrive, Marian ponders the concept of justice. Her mind wanders to Peter and his scientific "approach" to things and she wonders whether or not he has a "how-to" book for her. Marian watches him cut his meat and realizes the violence of the gesture. She imagines the cookbook pictures that display cows sectioned off according to different cuts of meat. She finds herself unable to finish her steak.

We next see Marian facing the reality of her situation, eating peanut butter, thumbing through a cookbook, and making a mental list of the food she is no longer able to eat. These include most meats, although hotdogs seem to be allowed. She is concerned about her protein levels and about becoming a vegetarian. By the end of the chapter, however, her difficulty with food has increased. She finds herself unable to eat her morning egg, an injunction prompted by Len's visit to the apartment the previous day. Len, stricken by guilt over impregnating the innocent Ainsley, comes to beg Marian to convince Ainsley to have an abortion. Marian reveals Ainsley's plot to him. Ainsley returns home and absolves Len of all responsibility. Len, in turn, explains that he's now emotionally involved and feels used. Marian feels disgusted by the whole thing and heads for bed.

Discomfort seems to be the primary emotion in the following chapter as well, which opens with the office Christmas party. Marian, because of her recent engagement, no longer fits in with the office social scene and its preoccupation with food and female topics. She scrutinizes the women at their party, thinking about the unflattering shapes of some of their bodies, feeling some awkwardness about her kinship with them. When Mrs. Bogue announces Marian's engagement and indicates she will soon be leaving her job as a result, Marian seems almost relieved. She certainly feels a sense of freedom and escape when she leaves the party. On the walk home, Marian runs into Duncan, who is sitting on a park bench. She sits with him, takes his hand, and snuggles inside his coat. He tells her he's been expecting her.

In the chapters that follow, Marian's eating disorder worsens. Remembering her Christmas visit to her parents, she recalls their pleasure at hearing the news of the wedding, together with their surprise that she couldn't eat any turkey. Now, while preparing a salad, she wonders whether the carrot she is slicing had screamed when it was uprooted, and she finds that carrots are now added to the list of forbidden foods. When organizing a dinner party to introduce Peter to Clara and Joe, Marian has difficulty coming up with something she can eat. The dinner party itself proves unsuccessful. Clara and Joe bring the children, Peter and Joe cannot make conversation comfortably, and Marian is uncomfortable when Clara changes a very messy diaper on the floor in front of them all. The chapter ends with Ainsley returning home from prenatal class concerned that her baby will be homosexual because of the lack of a strong father figure.

Although reluctant about the deception, Marian continues to see Duncan. While visiting the Royal Ontario Museum, she and Duncan exchange a kiss in the Egyptian room. When Duncan suggests that they sleep together, Marian refuses on the grounds of her engagement. Duncan responds that he needs sexual experience and that the wedding engagement is her problem. Marian seems less convinced with this shaky logic than with the fact that he is too self-absorbed to be badly hurt. She reasons that they are using each other. Consequently, she agrees to have dinner with Duncan and his roommates at their apartment that evening, but slips her engagement ring into her purse at the last moment. The dinner scene, which closely resembles the Mad Hatter's tea party in Lewis Carroll's *Alice in Wonderland* and is a comic highlight of the novel, takes place in chapter 22. Although ostensibly Duncan's roommates had invited Marian to dinner so that they could learn more about her, they dominate the conversation, competing for time and audience to present their ideas about literature. They are so absorbed in their own literary interpretations of Lewis Carroll's *Alice in Wonderland* that they do not notice how Marian tosses her pieces of meat to Duncan, who eats them for her. When Fish thumps the table for emphasis at the end of his speech, food and drinks spill everywhere, serving as an appropriate climax to the meal. When walking Marian home, Duncan reintroduces the idea of sleeping together. Although Marian agrees, they cannot find a suitable location at that time. Marian puts her engagement ring back on once she arrives at the subway station.

Perhaps prompted by Marian's encounter with the eccentric roommates over dinner, or perhaps by her increasing difficulties with food (by chapter 23, she has trouble even eating canned rice pudding), Marian has doubts about her own normalcy. Ainsley, when questioned on the subject, replies that nobody is normal. Clara, questioned on the same subject, puts Marian's difficulties down to bridal jitters. Peter assures Marian that she is normal. However, she can't eat the heart-shaped Valentine's cake she has bought for him. Peter, on the other hand, seems to experience no loss of physical or sexual appetite.

Chapters 24 and 25 involve preparations for a party Peter hosts before his wedding. Peter asks Marian to buy a nice dress and to have her hair styled. She purchases a tight red dress with sequins despite the fact that she doesn't think it suits her and then visits a salon. For her part, on the afternoon before Peter's party and again just before Peter collects her, Marian takes a vitamin pill to boost her energy. Her eating disorder has taken on frightening proportions. She avoids, for example, doing the dishes because she feels that perhaps the mold has a right to live too. She takes a bath and, as she watches three reflections of herself that appear on the bathtub fixtures, she begins to feel separated from her body, as if it no longer belonged to her. She combats this feeling by putting her engagement ring back on. Marian admits to herself that she's scared of losing control of her emotions at Peter's party, and she examines the two dolls she had meant to throw out earlier. (Clearly, she was unable to act upon the resolutions she made at the close of part 1.) Eventually, she invites some of her own friends to the party: Duncan and his roommates, Clara and Joe, as well as the office virgins. She puts on the girdle she was pressured into buying, followed by her red dress. Ainsley helps her with the zipper, lends her some earrings, and does her makeup and nails.

In both chapters, the party preparations are countered by the disintegration of Ainsley's relationship with Len, which foreshadows the impending breakup in Marian's own relationship. When Marian returns to her apartment from the hairdresser, she finds Ainsley and Len in the middle of an argument. Len is upset because Ainsley wants him to marry her. Len tries everything to shirk responsibility. He leaves, hurling insults at these particular women and at women in general. The landlady, alerted by the commotion, speaks out against Ainsley's immorality. Ainsley pushes back, accusing the landlady of hypocrisy and revealing the circumstances around her own pregnancy.

In chapter 26, as Peter and Marian put on the finishing touches for the party at Peter's apartment, the relationship has clearly reached a point of crisis from Marian's point of view. Peter, however, seems to feel quite differently. Peter is excited by Marian's choice of wardrobe and hair, but Marian, upon looking in a mirror, is barely able to recognize herself. Before the party, Peter asks her into his bedroom so that he may photograph her. After he arranges her in an artificial pose, Marian freezes, paralyzed with fear, in front of the camera.

The party itself begins in chapter 27 and rather than cementing established relationships, serves to undermine them.

The ominous nature of the party is signaled at its beginning when even Joe, the paradigm of a successful husband in this novel, admits to Marian that he has some doubts about how good marriage has been for Clara. He feels her role as a university-educated woman and her role as a wife and mother are diametrically opposed and that, as her husband, he's invading her "core" by placing her in a role that demands passivity. Joe wonders if perhaps it's a mistake for women to go to university at all.

Marian cannot respond because her attention is taken up with the commotion going on between Ainsley and Len, who arrives with Clara and Joe, both of whom are ignorant about who the woman behind his misery really is. Ainsley seems unperturbed by his arrival and even goes so far as to announce publicly that they are going to have a baby. Len responds by pouring beer over her head, and Fish rushes to her aid by mopping it up with his sweater. Throughout the fiasco, Peter snaps photographs.

The third relationship to crumble at the party is Marian's own. Her discomfort in her role as hostess and as Peter's fiancée is symbolized by her discomfort with the red dress. Duncan's comments upon first seeing her in it, that it makes the party seem like a "masquerade," don't help. When Peter points his camera at her, she shields herself and screams. Peter tells her she is drunk. Marian just feels panic and finally leaves the party, aware that her red dress makes her seem like a target. She heads toward the Laundromat, where Duncan went before having even met Peter, all the time conscious that Peter may be behind her.

When she finds Duncan in the Laundromat, she insists that they make love. Duncan scrapes up enough money for a cheap hotel room. When they find a hotel that will let them stay, because of the time of night and her appearance, the hotel clerk looks at Marian as if she were a prostitute. At first, Duncan seems more interested in Marian's girdle than in Marian. He insists she wash off her makeup before they make love. For the first half hour, their efforts are futile and Duncan claims all the flesh is making him feel smothered. Marian feels miserable, yet is determined to succeed. Finally they make love, and Duncan's face reminds Marian of an inquisitive animal who is not overly friendly.

The next morning Marian and Duncan go to a dingy coffee shop for breakfast. Marian is disgusted and unable to eat a morsel, while Duncan voraciously consumes a large breakfast. While Duncan gets up to leave, claiming he has to work on a paper, Marian begs him not to desert her. She does not want to go back to her apartment, and she especially dreads tackling the stack of dirty dishes that awaits her. At first, Duncan resists staying because it would imply involvement, but upon realizing how desperate Marian is, he changes his mind. Marian is unable to explain her behavior and feels that teaching Duncan about sex is all she's accomplished recently. She questions him about their encounter last night, seeking reassurance, only to find out that not only was she not Duncan's first lover but his reaction to her is barely lukewarm. She then asks Duncan to come back with her and help her talk to Peter. He refuses and disappears into the ravine. Marian heads for the subway.

Peter phones soon after Marian returns to her apartment. He is naturally upset with her and confused with her recent erratic behavior. He is also curious about Duncan. Marian suggests he come for tea that afternoon. She then heads to the supermarket and acquires all the necessary ingredients to make a sponge cake. Once the cake has been baked, she cuts it into the shape of a woman. Using icing, she then decorates it by adding a pink dress, shoes, lips, fingernails, and a face topped by a mass of brown curls. Marian feels slightly dismayed at the fact that her cake-woman will be eaten but accepts that as the inevitable fate of all food. When Peter arrives, Marian presents him with the cake and accuses him of trying to destroy her. She offers the cake as a "substitute." Peter looks at her in horror and leaves, quickly. Marian's appetite miraculously returns, and she begins to devour the cake, feet first. She feels a slight pang at having lost Peter, but she is not overly upset. Ainsley returns home with Fish and, seeing Marian eating the cake, accuses her of rejecting her femininity. Marian dismisses this as nonsense. However, since this is the closing comment of part 2, it does carry a certain weight.

Part 3 consists of only one chapter, which seems separated from the earlier chapters both in time, since it takes place two days later, and narrative style, since Marian uses "I" to narrate it. Marian finally begins to act on the resolutions, announced at the end of part 1, to tidy things up. She begins by cleaning the apartment. Duncan telephones her, eager to discuss Fish's marriage to Ainsley. Marian wants to talk about her broken engagement and her current job search. Duncan remarks that their roles as listener and talker have been reversed. However, when he does come for coffee he proceeds to talk about himself, focusing on how Fish's marriage and Trevor's response to it have affected him. Marian is concerned about Len, who is staying with Clara and Joe, refuses to go out, and fights with their children over toys. Duncan inquires about Marian's difficulty with food issues, and she proudly tells him about having eaten a steak. The novel ends with Duncan complicating who was trying to destroy whom. He first tells Marian that she was trying to destroy Peter, not vice versa, and that perhaps he, Duncan, had been trying to destroy her. However, he concludes by dismissing the whole issue because Marian is back to being a consumer herself. He eats the rest of the cake Marian offers him and tells her it's almost as good as Trevor's.

CHARACTER DEVELOPMENT

This novel centers on Marian and the changes in her character during a particular moment of crisis in her life. The other characters in the novel serve as foils who highlight specific qualities in Marian through comparison or contrast. At almost every turn, we are able to compare Marian's decisions, responses, and interpretations to those of the characters around her. Such points of comparison are particularly important in part 1 and part 3, where Marian tells her own story in the first-person singular (using "I" constructions). After all, in these sections, the reader's vision of the world is limited to Marian's increasingly distorted point of view.

The novel's central action revolves around Marian's heightening anxiety about her impending marriage and the simultaneous development of an eating disorder. At a time before the phrase "anorexia nervosa" was part of everyday speech (the disorder attracted special media attention in the past two decades), *The Edible Woman* documents the development of this condition. Since the eating disorder manifests itself in Marian's reaction to food, it is not surprising that the changes in Marian's character are traced through a sequence of food scenes in the novel.

If we look at the two food scenes that frame the novel—the first chapter's breakfast scene with Marian and Ainsley and the last chapter's cake scene—readers can see the dramatic changes that have taken place within Marian. In the novel's opening scenes, Marian is clearly the most reliable and rational of the two roommates. She is the one who mediates between the hotheaded Ainsley and the nosy landlady. She is the one who keeps a tidy room, pays for the scotch but seldom drinks it, and prefers not to be late for work. In the novel's closing chapters, however, when Marian prepares and serves a doll-shaped cake to Peter as a "substitute" for herself, Peter clearly interprets her actions as alarmingly neurotic. At one level, then, the novel documents Marian's journey from normalcy to neurosis.

However, readers can interpret this closing scene, indeed Marian's experience of an eating disorder, a bit differently if they come to sympathize with Marian's position. Atwood certainly invites readers to agree with Marian, up to a point. Most obviously, Marian seems quite right to see the world in which she lives as a consumer society based upon the sale and purchase of goods. After all, both she and Ainsley work in the corporate world. Marian's company, Seymour Surveys, documents consumer reactions to corporate advertising. Ainsley's job is to test defective electric toothbrushes. Where readers may begin to question Marian, however, is when her sympathies with food, and her perception of the threatening nature of the men around her that prompt this, lead her to health-threatening dysfunction.

Atwood, nevertheless, provides evidence throughout the novel that women do not fare well in their relationships with men. The institutions of marriage and motherhood reduce Clara, the novel's example of a married woman of Marian's age, to a near vegetable state. Is Joe not right when he explains that her "core" has been invaded, rather the way an apple can be destroyed by a worm? Marian herself feels particularly vulnerable when she is with Peter. There are three pivotal scenes in which Marian's discomfort grows. The first scene, over drinks at the Plaza Hotel with Len, documents Marian's disgust as she listens to their rather bloody account of a rabbit chase. Sympathizing with the rabbit, Marian first goes to the bathroom, later hides behind the couch, and finally tries to run away from Peter. In the second scene, over a steak dinner with Peter, Marian recognizes the savagery in the act of eating meat. She quickly identifies with the cow and finds herself unable to eat her own steak. Finally, at the engagement party, Marian feels that she herself has become the target of Peter's savagery. The camera Peter shoots at her all evening takes on the proportions of a gun, and she flees from the party feeling that, in her red dress, she resembles a shooting target that is being hunted. From Marian's point of view, this moment marks the beginning of her escape from Peter and her return to health. In her mind, when she offers him the doll-shaped cake as a substitute for the thing he wants to consume—herself—she has cleverly constructed a way out of her dilemma.

Another way to read the novel's closing scene is to see it as an example of Marian's predatory behavior. There are many female huntresses in this novel, women who actively pursue their men, and perhaps Marian can be seen as a consumer as well as one of the consumed. Ainsley is the most obvious example of the huntress, as she sets the trap for a surrogate father for her child, chases Len, and finally lands Fish as a husband. Lucy, one of the office virgins, is another huntress who, by choosing the posh restaurant for lunch, hopes to snag an eligible bachelor. However, all the office virgins, so intrigued with how Marian snagged Peter, perceive courtship as a ritual initiated by women.

At times, Marian plays a similar role in her fascination with and pursuit of Duncan during the encounters that frame their relationship. She (unknowingly) initiates the first encounter with Duncan, when she knocks on his door for the Moose Beer survey. Perhaps Duncan's interpretation of the symbolism of Marian's cake, that Marian has been trying to devour Peter, may not be so half-baked after all.

If the female characters serve as foils for Marian, then the male characters seem to serve as alternative choices for her. Peter (his name means "the rock" and suggests a certain stability), a law student in his articling year, offers the possibility of a respectable middle-class life. Duncan, the self-absorbed English graduate student who enjoys an almost childlike role in his life with roommates Fish and Trevor, offers a more ambiguous alternative. He seems to represent everything that Peter is not, and he appears in the chapters immediately following moments when Marian doubts her relationship with Peter.

Len Slank is a more minor figure in Marian's story. However, his interest in younger women and his fear of marriage and the responsibilities of fatherhood provide the novel with an example of a stereotypically confirmed bachelor. In comparison with Len, Peter seems very responsible, Joe (as the model of a solid husband and reliable father) even more so, and Duncan engagingly unpredictable. Although a minor character, Len consequently provides an important point of comparison for the men in this novel.

THEMATIC DEVELOPMENT

The Edible Woman critiques the kind of consumer society that dominated North America in mid- to late twentieth century, where relationships between individuals are built upon consumer relations and status is based upon purchasing power. The critique is largely a feminist one that aims to expose, and thereby dismantle, the way women are oppressed, used, or "consumed" in such a society. Consequently, the central character is a woman, and the novel documents the way she feels vulnerable to those around her: the male bosses at work and, most specifically, her fiancé, Peter. Seymour Surveys is described as an ice cream sandwich, where the (male) bosses occupy offices on the top floor and the women toil in the ranks below. Women are not expected to advance through the ranks of the company to management level in part because they are expected to leave the corporate world to raise a family. Mrs. Bogue announces at the Christmas office party that Marian will leave her job when she marries Peter. With the exception of the office manager, Mrs. Bogue, who works on the same floor as the employees she manages, we see no examples of women who have become corporate executives. Even the dentists that Ainsley meets at the party are described as male.

Not only is there an imbalance of power within the company, but the company itself surveys consumers in an effort to give corporations the upper hand by refining their products and marketing techniques. Seymour Surveys, in other words, is in the business of perpetuating a consumer society. Some of the funniest moments in this novel involve the surveys conducted by Seymour Surveys. They are some of the most pointed examples of the way individuals try to manipulate one another and also are hilariously funny because of the ways they go awry. Think here of the disastrous instant-tomato-juice survey conducted on a very stormy day, the coast-to-coast sanitary napkin survey that is accidentally mailed out to men and to 80-year-old women, and Marian's interview with Duncan on the subject of Moose Beer. In all cases, the interviewers lose control of the situation.

The novel uses exaggeration to reveal the power imbalances in society, comparing human relationships to the relationship between consumer and food, predator and prey. Marian's doll cake at the novel's close is the last and most explicit example of the close identification between people and food in this novel, but throughout the novel there are many instances when women are compared with food. At the office Christmas party, for example, Marian notices the unflattering shapes of the women's bodies. Mrs. Gundridge possesses a "ham-like bulge of thigh" (184) and "her jowls jellied when she chewed" (185). Moreover, all the coworkers are described as being either "ripe" or "overripe" as they are seen to be con-nected "by stems" to an "invisible vine" (184). Clara, when pregnant, seems like a vegetable. Marian finds herself identifying with the Valen-tine's cake she gives Peter, the steak they eat for dinner; and when she's getting her hair done for his party, her appearance—over which she feels she has little control—foreshadows the cake she later decorates—and can control.

Men in this novel are seldom compared with food. Rather, their role is that of consumer. Moreover, when women become predators, as when Ain-sley pursues Len, their prey is not described in terms of food. Such uneven treatment of the sexes in Atwood's fiction has been noted by her critics, who argue that her depictions of men are often more two-dimensional than three-dimensional. The publication of her most recent novel, *Oryx and Crake*, provides one direct rebuttal to such a charge. However, in such early novels as *The Edible Woman*, the charge that male characters seem rather flat and two-dimensional seems justified.

SOCIOHISTORICAL CONTEXT

The novel is set in Toronto of the 1960s and documents the career and marriage options of its protagonist, Marian MacAlpin. We don't know Marian's exact age, but she is a young woman in her twenties. Marian's fiancé, Peter, is 26 (69). Her roommate, Ainsley, is a few months older than she (72), and her coworkers, whom she calls the office virgins, are about her own age (21). Atwood has chosen the ages of her characters and the particular decade in which they live with care. The 1960s saw the first articulation of what would become a strident feminist movement in the 1970s, carrying Marian's generation of young women into a new era. Significant dates in the 1960s include: the Canadian Bill of Rights in 1960, the death of John F. Kennedy in 1963, the liberalization of Canadian laws in the late 1960s on abortion and homosexuality during Pierre Elliott Trudeau's term as justice minister in Canada, the 1968 Canadian federal government's appointment of the Royal Commission on the Status of Women, the legalization of the birth control pill in Canada one year later, and the popular fashion trend of the miniskirt and hot pants. Further, the publication of Betty Friedan's 1963 book *The Feminist Mystique* marked a turning point in women's perception of the value of their role as housewives and mothers. Giving the name "feminine mystique" to the predominant and hopelessly romanticized vision of the value of the stay-at-home housewife, Friedan gave voice to women's dissatisfaction with their postwar role in the home. After all, World War II had brought many women into the corporate and professional workforce. But the return of soldiers after the war meant that women were encouraged to return to the domestic sphere. Marian's ambivalence about the role of housewife that she is taking on reflects the growing ambivalence felt by many women across North America at the time. Ainsley, with her outspoken plan to conceive a child out of wedlock, is one example of the new wave of feminists. Ultimately, though, one must wonder what Atwood saying about the viability of such strident feminism when she has Ainsley decide to marry Fish and raise her child together with him. Perhaps this is one of many moments in the novel when Atwood, although clearly a feminist, parodies, or exaggerates in order to poke fun at, aspects of the very philosophy she espouses. In moments of humorous exaggeration, *The Edible Woman* provides a parody of feminism in much the same way as the searingly funny *Lady Oracle* parodies the gothic.

Although eating disorders are documented long before the twentieth century, anorexia nervosa was not widely discussed in the popular media until the 1970s. By documenting so closely the development of an eating disorder, Atwood anticipates what would soon become a central focus and concern of North American society. Ironically, by locating the source of this disorder in Marian's identification with food, Atwood also points to a longstanding literary tradition of comparing women with food. Literary critic Eira Patnaik writes that "from time immemorial the female has been identified with edible commodities. For the Elizabethans it was almost cliché to compare her complexion with whipped cream, her cheeks with ripening peaches and her lips with red cherries. Similarly, the Middle-East has identified her with a veritable banquet of exotic delights: her cheeks are pomegranates; her lips luscious grapes" (59). Patnaik goes on to explain a theory that coincides with Joe's own theory about his wife Clara (that she is like an apple that is gradually losing its "core") as he presents it to Marian at Peter's bachelor party. Patnaik argues that his explanation that women are perceived as food supports "the theory, prevalent well into the nineteenth century, that women have no core. They are matter, bereft of soul or essence, while man is mind, endowed with the highest worth of existence" (65). That, in the case of *The Edible Woman*, the comparison between women and food is experienced rather than articulated, and perceived from a woman's point of view, turns the tables entirely. This shift in dynamic is a feminist one, designed to expose the way such a tradition belittles the women it purports to praise.

NARRATIVE TECHNIQUE

Although the narrative structure (or ordering of events) is remarkably linear, since it systematically follows Marian's experiences from the beginning of the crisis through to its end, the narrative technique (or portrayal of events) is more complicated. *The Edible Woman* is divided into three parts: the first part comprises chapters 1 through 12, the middle section consists of chapters 13 through 30, and the third and concluding section consists merely of chapter 31. It is interesting to note that the narrative voice switches in each part. The first part is told in the first person; Marian, the protagonist, or main character, refers to herself as "I." The second part changes to omniscient third-person narration, where Marian's actions are recounted by an all-knowing (omniscient) third-person narrator using the pronoun "she." And the final chapter and third part of the novel returns once more to the first-person voice.

Why does Atwood shift the voice to the third person for the second part of the novel? One answer is that it performs in the narrative precisely what Marian experiences during those chapters: a separation between her mind and her body, between her decisions and the decisions her body makes for her, especially about what she can and cannot eat. Another related answer is that the third-person narrative gives control of Marian's story to someone other than Marian herself. Of course, this is precisely what Marian feels is happening in her engagement with Peter, and it puts her at a disadvantage: she has relinquished control over her relationship to Peter. In both cases, the narrative technique mirrors what is happening in the text. When Marian regains control over her state of mind, in part 3, it seems entirely appropriate that she also regains control over her own story. The return to first-person narration coincides with the reintegration of Marian's mind and body, and with Marian's return to her original position at the beginning of the novel—she is orderly (and is, finally, doing the tidy-up she has planned), single, and a consumer.

A BIOGRAPHICAL READING

Although some critics, including T. D. MacLulich and Sharon Wilson, argue that *The Edible Woman* is a modern-day reworking of traditional fairy tales, most see this novel as a feminist critique of the way society marginalizes women, even in the late twentieth century. This study is no exception. However, publications of the past few years have made available sufficient evidence for a strong biographical reading of the novel, one that complements the dominant feminist reading. Biographical readings explore the text in relation to the environment in which it was written in order to trace the way in which the text reproduces, exaggerates, or reconstructs events, as well as attempt to explain why it does so. In some ways, of course, this is also the goal of a historicist perspective. However, whereas a historicist perspective focuses on the relationship between the text and events in the public sphere (so-called historical events taking place on the municipal, regional, national, or world stage, for example), a biographical reading focuses on the relationship between the text and events in the private sphere of the author's own life and experiences.

Although *The Edible Woman* was written on exam booklets in 1965, while Atwood was teaching courses at the University of British Columbia, it draws heavily upon the details surrounding her experience working for Canadian Facts Marketing at the corner of Bay and Wellington in Toronto from the summer of 1963 until the spring of 1964. Atwood was hired to fact-check and edit the survey questionnaires, and she was at Canadian Facts during the heyday of consumer testing, the era of Tang and Pop Tarts. The work environment at Seymour Surveys is very similar to that of Canadian Facts, the ladies working at one end of the floor, the office managers upstairs. As in the novel, during breaks, Atwood and her coworkers would head across Bay Street to the Mercury Café for coffee and Danish pastries. Two of her coworkers at the time see a resemblance to themselves in the depictions of Lucy and Emmy. In a letter to me,

Atwood's boss at Canadian Facts introduced herself as "Mrs. Bogue" (Sims). There are other characters developed from those in Atwood's life. For example, Peter is a fictionalized version of Atwood's boyfriend, and later fiancé, Jay (James) Ford. The two were engaged in August of 1963, when Atwood was working at Canadian Facts Marketing, and his Christmas present to her was an engagement ring. The engagement was broken off by Easter of 1964. Although he was a philosophy graduate student rather than a lawyer, Ford was, like Peter in the novel, an amateur photographer. Ford remembers that Atwood wrote to him as she began writing the novel, asking him not to "take this personally" (Cooke, Interview with Ford). Similarly, Atwood contacted the Mrs. Bogue character to explain that she didn't really think of her as such a "Helen Hokinson" type, meaning an earnest and rather tiresomely serious person. On the contrary, the model for Mrs. Bogue more closely resembles another Atwood character she inspired: the wonderful Aunt Lou of *Lady Oracle.* Quite rightly, Ford did not "take it personally." He, like the real-life counterparts of Lucy, Emmy, and Mrs. Bogue, fully understood that characters must be exaggerated and distorted to suit the comic and thematic purposes of the novel. Fiction can never be too close to life.

Ironically, there are a couple of examples to suggest that art can anticipate life. In 1987, for example, Atwood explained that, at the time of writing *The Edible Woman,* she had never heard of anorexia. Marian's eating disorder, which is sometimes used as a case study since it provides such close scrutiny of Marian's changing state of mind, and has prompted numerous letters to Atwood from anorexics, was therefore prompted by "symbolic" rather than physiological conditions ("Who Created Whom"). Another reminder of the way fictional creations can approximate reality occurred when Atwood discovered that there really was a Moosehead Beer, a close approximation of the Moose Beer in the novel.

The biographical context can provide more than an explanation of various correspondences between life and fiction, however. In this case, the feminist impulse behind the novel can be traced to events in 1963 and 1964, years that proved formative to Atwood as a feminist. By the time Atwood worked at Canadian Facts in 1963, she had already been exposed to what we now call "empowering" feminist influences. Atwood came from a family with a number of particularly strong female role models. Her mother, for example, was a good shot and not only kept the family fed but also safe from bears and predators during the seasons they spent in the bush with Atwood's entomologist father. Her maternal aunts were made of equally strong mettle: one graduated with an MA in history from the University of Toronto at the age of 19, then married and had six children. The other, Joyce Barkhouse, had two children and has become a biographer and, as the author of the very popular children's novel *Pit Pony*, a best-selling children's writer.

Atwood was exposed to more strong women during her undergraduate years at the University of Toronto's Victoria College. Unlike some of the other colleges at the university, Victoria's faculty included women. One faculty member called Jay Macpherson, herself a Canadian poet, was a particularly strong influence. Indeed, the style of Atwood's first poetry chapbook, *Double Persephone*, reveals the influence of Macpherson's own work. As well, the classroom atmosphere at Victoria College encouraged women to engage in vigorous debate. Consequently, when Atwood began graduate studies at Radcliffe College, she was understandably shocked to find herself excluded, as a woman, from certain library facilities (the Lamont Library in particular) and expected to serve coffee and cookies to the male students during the mid-class break in Victorian Humor.

The Atwood who joined Canadian Facts, then, was already sensitized to issues of gender equality. That sensitivity would be transformed into a resolve over the next two years, prompted by three things.

First, at Canadian Facts Marketing, Atwood was exposed to more evidence about the unequal treatment of women in the workplace: the expectation that young women would leave work when they married; that women should be paid less than their male counterparts, in part because the latter were supporting families; and the insubstantial opportunities for promotion in a company structure that, literally and figuratively, kept the male executives on the top. All three of these inequalities became apparent as she watched various coworkers challenge them—one by asking for a raise, another by struggling to support four children on the salary she earned (Cooke, Interview with Lloyd).

Next, Atwood's boss at Canadian Facts was a committed member of the NDP (National Democratic Party), had a strongly feminist bias, and explicitly encouraged her to become more involved in political activism. Atwood's response in 1963 was that she was devoting an enormous amount of energy to her writing and had little additional capacity (Sims, Letter). At the time she was working at Canadian Facts, she was also writing her first novel: *Up in the Air So Blue*. By the following year, however, as she wrote the first draft of *The Circle Game*, which was more assertively feminist than the later published version, and when she wrote *The Edible Woman*, Atwood began to use her writing *as* political, and explicitly feminist, activism.

most written-about Canadian writer ever, and there is an enormous amount of academic criticism on her work produced not only in North America, but also in Britain, and increasingly in Europe, Australia and India" (6).

PLOT DEVELOPMENT

Reminiscent of Jack Kerouac's classic 1957 American novel, *On the Road* (a title that Atwood, literally, echoes in the novel's first line), the opening of *Surfacing* describes the narrator's journey, by car, back through the landscape of her childhood. Kerouac's novel traces the path of the writer and narrator Sal Paradise, who travels endlessly throughout the United States and Mexico meeting up with a drifter, Dean Moriarty, and various girlfriends along the way. While the novel can be read as one of male self-discovery, it also highlights a riotous, youthful lifestyle of drinking, freedom, and mobility. The allusion or reference to Kerouac's novel is deliberate on Atwood's part. *Surfacing* takes up a similar story of self-discovery, but tells it not only from the point of view of a woman, but also from the point of view of a *Canadian* woman.

The unnamed narrator and main character of Atwood's novel finds herself traveling by car with her boyfriend, Joe, and two friends, David and Anna, on a road along which she traveled frequently as a child. She recognizes signs of development, like the new gravel road to the lake and other things that have changed over the years. There are signals, too, that the narrator has experienced significant changes as well. First, the Surfacer (the name here given to the novel's narrator) recalls how at a party Anna read her palm and noticed a "funny break" in her lifeline after her childhood. Second, Anna is the narrator's closest female friend, though they've only known each other for two months.

David and Joe are making a movie called *Random Samplings,* which, as the film's name suggests, involves their shooting footage at relatively random moments. As with Peter's amateur photography in *The Edible Woman,* the narrator becomes increasingly uncomfortable with the kind of control the camera seems to give them and the lack of control experienced by the women, who are expected to remain on the other side of the lens. (This discomfort is felt both by Marian at Peter's party and with Anna's humiliation, later on in *Surfacing,* at being filmed naked.) Some of the signposts on this road are familiar to Canadians who have traveled in northern Ontario toward the Quebec border: the house made from pop bottles and the stuffed moose dressed in human clothing, still visible north of Hunts-ville, Ontario, on Highway 11.

In chapter 2, we learn that the Surfacer is on a quest or mission to find out what has happened to her father, who has vanished mysteriously despite being an experienced woodsman. We also learn more about the recent changes in the Surfacer's life that were signaled or foreshadowed in the opening section. While the others go for beer, the Surfacer talks to one of her father's friends, Paul, in her best classroom French (they have crossed the border into Quebec). Paul's wife, yet another woman in this novel who remains nameless because she is known only as "Madame," extends sympathies on the death of the Surfacer's mother and asks the Surfacer if she has brought her husband. Rather than mention the divorce and explain that Joe is not her husband, she lies. Luckily, she thinks, Ma-dame didn't ask about the baby.

We learn a little more about the "baby" in the next chapter when the Surfacer talks to a childhood companion, Claude. She explains that her parents understood her divorce less than her marriage, and they don't forgive her for "leaving her child," although she claims it did not really belong to her. Claude arranges for an American, Evan, to give them a boat ride to the cottage. During the trip there, she watches Evan closely, clearly distrustful of him. When they arrive, she sees the dock where her brother almost drowned. Although her mother was pregnant with her when it happened, she claims she saw it through her mother's stomach "like a frog in a jar" (32). This is the first example of a kind of intuitive sense of kinship between the Surfacer and the landscape around her.

By contrast, there are numerous signs of the Surfacer's alienation from people. In chapter 4, she examines the cottage and interprets the swing and fence as a sign of failure on her part. That everything is in order and that there are no messages for her make it all the more poignant. She claims that the child was not hers, that it was "imposed" on her by her husband. Significantly, it has been nine years since she's been here. Sym-bolically, the reader wonders whether the number nine, the same number for months in a pregnancy, foreshadows the possibility of a rebirth of her relationship with her parents. Nine years is also the length of time David and Anna have been married, though the Surfacer wonders how the mar-riage has lasted so long. Although she has clearly invited David and Anna to join her on this trip, she seems uncomfortable in their presence. During conversation after dinner, for example, she finds it difficult to laugh at David's extremist remarks. He says Canada would be fine without the "fascist pig Yanks and the capitalists" and suggests attack beavers as a means for elimination.

One explanation for the Surfacer's sense of alienation is that she seems to be fighting worry and loss on a number of different fronts. However, in chapter 5 it becomes clear that she seems to have difficulty in most of her relationships with men, including her current one with Joe. She thinks that, while he's a good lover, reserved and convenient, he is moody and really doesn't mean that much to her. She blames this on her divorce, which she compares to an amputation. However, it seems she is the one who performed the amputation. While walking through the bush, the Surfacer remembers how charming her husband used to be. She wonders why she is now so bitter given that she was the one who left him. He had just wanted a solid marriage and a child. The Surfacer also notices cracks in the relationship between David and Anna. Anna applies makeup each morning, at David's request. Without it, she looks "battered." When the Surfacer asks Anna why her marriage is successful, she cryptically replies that you have to make an "emotional commitment" and just "let go" (47). The Surfacer claims her marriage didn't work because she was "too young" (48). She doesn't correct Anna when she says it's fortunate there were no children.

In chapter 6, the Surfacer almost leaves the cottage, thinking that she has performed the necessary search and now wants to get back to her job in the city. The Surfacer works as a commercial artist/illustrator, and she unsuccessfully tries to sketch a princess for a book called *Quebec Folk Tales*. She recalls how her husband told her she should do something useful, since there were no great women artists. The Surfacer is the first of a series of novels whose central characters are female artists. However, this aspect of the Surfacer's identity is not developed at great length in this novel. Rather, she serves as a precursor for such figures as Joan in *Lady Oracle* and Elaine in *Cat's Eye*, novels that focus on the role of the female artist. Here, her job as illustrator (an applied art) is contrasted with Joe's craft. As a potter who deliberately mangles his pots, shaping them in impractical ways, Joe is an example of an artist who refuses to make his art functional.

Her father turns out to be an artist of sorts as well. However, his art—sketches and random words found on a stack of papers at the cottage—are not only impractical, but also seem indecipherable. At first the Surfacer is bewildered. She had never entertained the idea that her father may have gone mad, but now she is convinced that he is mad or bushed and vows to burn the drawings and respect his privacy. Alarmed that he may be roaming the island, she insists that they all join her on the fishing expedition after dinner. The Surfacer baits the hooks and kills the fish. Then they hear a motor and see what seem to be two Americans roar by in a flag-draped boat. One throws his cigar in the water, and the other vows to go to Florida due to the lack of fish. When asked, the Surfacer tells them that they hadn't caught any fish either. Her familiarity with the landscape is obviously not something these men share, nor something she wants to share with them.

Indeed she becomes increasingly introspective, daily activities triggering memories of her childhood. When she prepares fish for breakfast, for example, a task her father or brother would usually have done, her thoughts turn to her brother. He has also left and explores mineral rights on the other side of the world. While in the outhouse, she remembers the childhood difficulties that came with dividing her time between here and the city and with changing schools frequently. She felt alienated at birthday parties and on the playground. Throughout this chapter, David's intrusions make him seem almost like one of the Americans. At breakfast, he films the fish guts for *Random Samples*. Chapter 8 ends as the Surfacer swims away from David into the icy lake where her brother almost drowned. Consequently part 1 of this novel ends with the Surfacer submerging herself under the water, rather the way her return to the island of her childhood has submerged her in her childhood memories.

Part 2, which spans chapters 9 through 19, establishes a clear distinction between the Surfacer and those around her, people she will begin to think of as "Americans." It opens with the Surfacer wondering when she first noticed the difference between her friends (and "what they are turning into") and herself (76). Their canned laughter and robotic movements seem shallow to her. Unlike them, she feels trapped on the island, and she feels watched by her father. Although David has convinced her to let them stay on for a bit, she would prefer to leave. Joe tries to talk to her, but David interrupts by suggesting they chop wood. The Surfacer weeds the garden with Anna, keeping an eye open for her father. She remembers the days when they lived here in tents and her mother scared off a bear while their father was away. She and Anna talk about the drawbacks of the birth control pill. The Surfacer's mind drifts to her abortion, how powerless and alone she felt during the procedure. Her husband wasn't there with her, although he came to collect her afterwards.

The Surfacer becomes increasingly introspective and protective of her past. She doesn't want her father, whom she now assumes to have gone mad, to reappear. She feels she has to protect them from him, and him from them. She begins to feel threatened by the other men around her as well. Joe, for example, wants her to marry him. She refuses, saying that they are practically married already and telling him of her prior marriage and child. He argues their relationship would be different. She claims she's not good enough for Joe, who promptly gives her the cold shoulder. In this chapter, men in general seem to have tendencies that discomfit the Surfacer. When she finds her old scrapbooks, she notices that hers are different from her brother's: his is more violent in nature. Her brother's contains pictures of fighting and war; hers contain magazine cutouts of ladies, pretty dresses, and a series of happy rabbits and Easter eggs. She hides them under her mattress for safekeeping.

Greater threats emerge as other men approach the island in chapter 11. The sound of a motor announces the arrival of Paul and another man, Bill Malmstrom, from Detroit Michigan, a member of the Wildlife Protection Association of America. He is interested in purchasing the island and using it as a "retreat" spot for members. The Surfacer refuses, despite his generous offer. She later confides to Paul that she refused the offer because her father is still alive. Paul is skeptical. When David hears of the purchase offer, he launches into a big speech about the "pig Yanks" and the war over freshwater he envisions them starting in the future. David's behavior in this chapter, in the violence of his language here and in his later flirtations with the Surfacer, make him seem more foe than friend to the Surfacer, more "American" within the terms of this novel. While doing dishes, Anna explains that David is only flirting with her so that he can upset Anna. It's a sick game he plays because he has trouble remaining monogamous. Anna is hurt by his infidelity and how he flaunts it. The Surfacer is uncomfortable.

Chapter 12 destabilizes the Surfacer's interpretation of her relationships with the men around her and forces her to come to terms with her own emotional dysfunction. She tries talking with Joe, who remains hostile to her. She can't tell him whether or not she loves him, and he is convinced she thinks he's not good enough for her. While examining the papers with the drawings, she comes across letters from an academic indicating that her father's drawings are not a madman's doodles but merely sketches of rock drawings. This discovery makes her realize that her father isn't insane and alive, but that he is dead. She discovers that the numbers on the pictures correspond with the map hanging in one of the bedrooms. She wants to go to the areas he's marked off on the map, just to be sure. She figures she can convince David, who continues to make advances on her, to take her under the guise of fishing. The chapter ends with the Surfacer searching through an old photo album. She is no longer preoccupied with her father's death. Rather, she wants to discover when her own emotional death occurred. She finds no clues.

Like the Surfacer, readers search for clues about what traumatic event has affected the Surfacer. It seems to have something to do with the men and the threats they pose. After all, the Surfacer feels threatened by the most benign Joe and decides that she will move out when they go back to the city. However, the Surfacer also alienates herself from women. In chapter 13, for example, she refuses to stand up for Anna when she starts to defend herself against David. Clearly something is wrong, but exactly what and when it began remain unclear. However, this chapter, at the very center of the novel, provides a symbol for the kind of decay that characterizes the Surfacer's emotional state. As they cross a portage on their canoe trip, they encounter the rotting corpse of a dead heron, strung upside down in a tree. Who killed the heron? There are a number of possibilities: perhaps the two men with chainsaws who appear on a portage, or perhaps the Americans who mistake David's cry of "pigs" for a greeting.

David and Joe insist on filming the heron. Seeing it damaged and brutalized makes the Surfacer resent whoever had the audacity to kill it, and she believes it was the Americans. After dinner, all but Anna go fishing. They catch a fish easily this time. The Surfacer makes David kill it. She can't bring herself to kill it because they have brought more than enough food with them and they don't need it. To compensate, she frees one of the frogs she had brought as bait. They encounter two Americans and have a conversation about fishing. The Surfacer thinks about stories she's heard over the years about Americans exploiting the Canadian wilderness: about the men who tried to smuggle 200 trout over the border and those who killed loons for amusement. The Surfacer begins to see a parallel between the Americans' treatment of the wilderness and men's treatment of women. When Joe announces that he would like to stay with the Surfacer, even if unmarried, she refuses his offer. She further suggests that Anna leave David. She is disturbed by the arbitrary rules he makes up for her to follow (like wearing makeup), enforced through his withholding of sex. In later chapters, readers will agree with the Surfacer, as they watch David coerce Anna into posing nude for the film he's making. David's defense of his behavior is weak. He grumbles that Anna is not his intellectual equal, that she is unfaithful to him, and that he was trapped into marrying her. Clearly, filming her naked is a way for David to get back at her for his longstanding and deep-seated feelings of resentment toward her.

That "American" comes to represent threatening and thoughtless behavior rather than a national affiliation is confirmed in chapter 15, when the Surfacer's group runs into "the Americans" once more and learns that they are actually Canadian. The Surfacer thinks about mankind's evil deeds and concludes that although Hitler is dead, the potential for evil still exists, and it can exist in anyone. (This is a theme often treated in Atwood's poetry. Examples include "It Is Dangerous to Read Newspapers" and "Trainride, Vienna-Bonn.") Although she and her brother didn't participate in playground cruelty at school, in the wilderness they still destroyed things: her doll, the burned leeches. She recalls when she freed all the animals her brother kept in jars in a laboratory and how angry he was. She wanted the world to look like her scrapbook: rabbits and Easter eggs, not like his, warlike and brutal. Upon returning, she sees the spot where surveyors have been and refers to Canada as "sold or drowned" (132).

The Surfacer realizes that the rock drawings have been submerged by the rising water levels, so she must dive into the lake to find them. This dive is both literal, since she takes the canoe out alone and jumps into the water, and figurative, since it marks the beginning of her getting to the bottom of what is troubling her. It takes her four tries to find it, but rather than a rock drawing it turns out to be her father's drowned body. In a literal sense, the mystery has been solved. After confronting this vision, she looks up to the surface of the water and notices two canoes. Both literally and symbolically, then, she is no longer alone. Joe has come to find her. Exhausted after the exertion, she lies at the bottom of the canoe. Joe keeps asking her if she's okay, but she can't respond because her mind is far away. He tries to make love to her but she refuses, thinking to herself that it would be a "sacrilege" because he is one of the "killers" (147). She warns him she'll get pregnant if they make love. Visions of her aborted child flash before her eyes. She recalls how the procedure was performed in a house, not a hospital. Her "husband" did not accompany her, having to attend a birthday party for his own children. The abortion is why she could no longer face her parents, could not tarnish their "perilous innocence" (144). Her "husband" had forced her to have the abortion, and she now feels guilty, like a murderer. She leaves her sweatshirt as a token for the nature gods, to acknowledge them and to compensate for her past. She figures her father must have known about them too, and the markings on the map showed where these "oracles" could be located (145). Did her mother leave a memento for her as well, she wonders?

Everyone else seems unaware of the delicate balance of nature and the power in it. She sees Americans in a powerboat heading toward the cliff, oblivious of her drowned father and the rock drawings. In a similar way, David approaches her, unaware of her past. When she refuses him, he tells her that Joe is sleeping with Anna. At dinner, the atmosphere is tense. David accuses her of hating men or of "want[ing] to be one" (154). She realizes that she hates "Americans," or what that term has come to represent for her.

The opposite of being an "American" seems to be someone who is conscious of the natural world and his or her place in it, like her father and her mother. This recognition provides the Surfacer with a path toward healing in the last chapter of part 2.

The same chapter brings the Surfacer's quest for her parents to a close. First, a boat approaches to announce that her father's body has been found. Some Americans hooked it while fishing. They explain that he had fallen from a cliff and the camera weighed him down in the water. The Surfacer keeps to herself her own interpretation of the circumstances surrounding his death. Next, she finds the gift left to her by her mother. It's in one of the scrapbooks, a picture of a pregnant woman with the baby peering out from her stomach that she herself had drawn as a child. Beside her is a horned man with a tail. The Surfacer brings her new insight to bear on the image, interpreting it for this particular stage in her life. She thinks, now, that Joe may be saved. So while the others imagine her full of death and grief, she has actually come to a new vision of life. She has begun to surface, in other words, from the depth of despair and dysfunction.

Part 3 signals this transformation when she joins Joe in bed and initiates sexual intercourse. He is surprised, especially when she insists they have sex outside. She urgently pulls him toward her, sensing it's the right time to conceive. Very quickly, she senses her "lost child" within her again and silently vows to give birth to this child, rather than to abort the fetus. This time, too, the birth will be a natural one. She imagines having the baby alone and in the wilderness, never teaching it spoken language. Joe tells her his lovemaking with Anna meant nothing and asks if she still loves him. She doesn't answer.

Having resolved her relationship with Joe, she sets out to neutralize David's antagonistic relationship with Anna and the world around him. Particularly provoking is David's suggestion that he and the Surfacer have sex in front of the camera since *Random Samples* has no sex footage. While David and Joe are putting the first canoe back, she unwinds the film and puts it in the lake. Anna watches her in disbelief and warns her of the consequences. David is devastated when Anna tells him, but by then the Surfacer has taken the second canoe and slipped away. She guides the canoe along the shoreline, hiding from them. They call her name (although the name itself isn't revealed to the reader) but as far as she's concerned, she no longer has a name. They get into the boat without her, and she considers them all to be Americans.

Finally alone, she begins to plan what she will need to survive. Since the tool shed and cabin are locked, she has to break a window to get back inside. They have left her stuff on the table inside, so she unpacks it, finds some peaches to eat and then falls into a deep sleep. When she wakes, though, she does not feel invigorated. Rather, it seems as though the power and insight she had felt earlier have disappeared. She cries in despair, furious with her parents for leaving her but wonders whether she can will them to come back. She screams "I'm here," but the silence scares her (172). She believes she can will them back; she can sense their presence. She tries to barricade herself in the cabin and spends the night battling fear. She can sense her parents trying to get in, and she prepares herself for seeing them again because they will have changed.

By morning, when she tries to brush her hair, she notices that the power seems to have returned. The brush seems forbidden to her. She concludes that there is a set of rules to follow. She is not allowed on the dock. She goes back to the cabin and burns her drawings and *Quebec Folk Tales* (the book she was illustrating), as well as her art supplies. She adds to the fire: her ring (from her "husband"), the scrapbooks, the wilderness guides, the map, her father's stack of papers, her mother's photo album, and a page from her father's books. She then breaks the dishes and the lamp. All things she is unable to break are thrown on the floor. She slashes any clothing and blankets. She takes with her only one slashed blanket until, as she describes it, "the fur grows" (177). She sheds her clothes in the lake. A loon eyes her, but considers her to be part of the landscape. She realizes she is hungry, but cannot eat anything in tins so she eats some raw beans and carrots. She makes herself a "lair" of leaves and branches and tries to sleep.

By the next chapter, she finds that she cannot even enter the garden. Enclosed spaces are problematic. So she resorts to eating raspberries and some mushrooms and imagines that she has given up the need for language. Then she seems to see her mother, wearing her leather jacket and feeding the birds. The mother turns, but doesn't actually seem able to see her, and then vanishes. Did she sense the Surfacer's fear? The Surfacer runs to where she had stood but sees only the blue jays and wonders which one of them her mother has become.

So removed from the world has she become that she hears the sounds but cannot understand the words spoken by those who come to the island in a powerboat. Fearful that they will trap her like the heron, she explodes in irrepressible laughter. When they hear it, they give chase, but she is able to evade them, moving quickly without shoes through the bushes. However, she pays for her speed in scratches and pains. Worse, toward the end she realizes that she is no longer allowed to use paths, or to use anything touched by metal. The reward for this new insight is a vision of her father, whom she sees standing looking at the garden. When he turns, though, he is not her father but what he must have become, a wolf-like creature, rather like the werewolves in the *Quebec Folk Tales*. As with the vision of her mother, the Surfacer rushes to where it had stood after its disappearance. What she finds, though, are her own footprints.

When she wakes the next morning, she knows that her parents have left. Gone too are the rules and, seemingly, some of what might be described as her madness. Once back in the cabin, surprised at the mess she made, she slowly eats a tin of beans. She realizes she can't stay too long, due to lack of food. She realizes that, although she'll have to return to the city and face the Americans, she should deal with them rather than fear or imitate them. She looks at herself in the mirror and realizes she looks like a woman gone mad.

In the book's final chapter, the Surfacer dresses in her damaged clothes. Feeling like a "time-traveller" (191) she brings back to her own world her unborn child. While she's in the garden, Paul and Joe arrive in a boat. Joe calls her name. She watches him from behind a tree, and realizes that if she joins him, she'll have to adopt language again and their relationship will likely fail. But, she acknowledges that he isn't an American, he's "half-formed" and this trait enables her to trust him (192). He calls her again, growing impatient, but for the time being he waits. The novel ends with the Surfacer listening to Joe, deciding whether to go back with him or not.

CHARACTER DEVELOPMENT

Although we never learn the central protagonist's name, her inner turmoil is developed in detail during the three sections of this novel. In part 1, we see her interactions with her partner and friends during a time of stress. Not only do we learn that some traumatic event has triggered a significant change in her character, and a disruption in her relationship with her parents, but we also begin to learn the nature of that event, an abortion. Part 2 establishes the source for the narrator's anxiety, a feeling of having been victimized in her earlier relationship. Consequently, the Surfacer develops a strong dislike of those she perceives as victimizers—men and those who come to be called "Americans"—and a sympathy for those she perceives as victims—the dead heron, frogs used as bait, Anna. Her own aborted fetus is one of the victims, of course, which makes her a victimizer as well. Consequently, she feels a deep ambivalence about what she perceives as a murder. As a result, when she finds her father's drowned body, she confronts a number of different ghosts from her past. If we watch the Surfacer dive into the heart of her trauma in part 2, then we watch her struggle toward the surface in part 3. This struggle involves a shamanistic experience. The shaman, or visionary, was expected to undergo a purification ritual that involved spending time alone and foregoing such bodily comforts as food and shelter in order to prepare himself to receive his vision. Similarly, the Surfacer finds herself required to forego a number of things and, rather like the shaman's prized spiritual insight (or is it the result of madness of the kind described in Atwood's poem, "Progressive Insanities of a Pioneer"), she finds herself rewarded by a vision of each one of her parents.

Whether she actually sees the ghosts of her parents is uncertain. In the tradition of such ghost stories as Henry James's *Turn of the Screw,* the reader is never entirely sure whether the ghosts exist or are figments of the perceiving character's imagination. Atwood does provide a rational explanation for these visions: stress and lack of food and clothing might account for the Surfacer's unusual frame of mind, not to mention the questionable nature of the mushrooms she eats. That the Surfacer finds her own footprints where the vision of her father once stood also suggests that she is herself the werewolf she has seen. In any case, the Surfacer does seem to find a sense of resolution through the rituals she performs. She placates her conscience, if not the gods, by ruining David's film and by conceiving a child with Joe. As well, she finds a way to make peace with her parents. Is this enough to restore her to health? The novel does not make the answer clear. Leaving the Surfacer hidden behind the tree, we are unsure whether she will return to the city. Further, were she to return, would she be able to significantly change her life's path?

Atwood has been criticized for not developing her characters very fully in this novel (Elliott, Fraser). In Joe's case, however, it is appropriate that he is only half-developed as a character. After all, that is precisely his role in this novel: he is a man whose character is still open to change. He proves willing to accommodate the Surfacer as she journeys through the emotional minefield in this novel.

David is another male character is this novel who is a flat, rather than a rounded or fully developed, character. He is a foil to Joe: whereas Joe says very little in the novel, David says too much; whereas Joe seems shaggy, already possessing the "fur" that the Surfacer thinks she will need to survive the elements, David spends his time combing his hair to hide the ever-increasing bald spot. Although David seems to have difficulty communicating sensitively with others, especially his wife, he ironically teaches "Communications." We know relatively little of David's past life (when he was studying for the ministry), and his present character is cobbled together from popular culture: his Woody Woodpecker laugh (chapter 16) and cliché comments about "Yanks" and "pigs." Indeed, David's outrage at Americans, and the language he uses to describe them, makes him seem more like a caricature than a three-dimensional character at all. Given his anti-American stance, it is ironic that his character derives from American popular culture. Driven by pride and conceit, David himself comes to embody what this novel defines as "American."

His wife, Anna, is not developed much more fully. However, we do overhear conversations between Anna and the Surfacer that provide glimpses into the way she is thinking. Although unhappy in her relationship with David and uncertain of herself, she remains loyal to her husband. If the Surfacer sees the unhealthiness of her relationship to David, she is unable to prompt Anna to action beyond the feminist comments she makes in chapter 13. By not supporting Anna's initiative at that moment, the Surfacer undermines Anna's trust in their friendship and perhaps in friendship between women more generally. Consequently, when the Surfacer later dumps the film in the lake, although Anna cannot stop her in time, she does tell on her to David.

THEMATIC DEVELOPMENT

Surfacing extends the exploration of feminist concerns begun in Atwood's two earlier book-length publications, *The Edible Woman* (a novel) and *The Circle Game* (poetry). Also, her poem "At the Tourist Center in Boston," included in the collection *The Animals in That Country*, treats Atwood's fear of what would happen to an Americanized Canada. This poem, like *Surfacing*, shifts between a wry, dark treatment of tourists and genuine concern about their impact on the environment.

Surfacing traces the Surfacer's increasing discomfort with a world that seems to be divided between victims and victimizers. Until the last chapter, the Surfacer sees herself as a victim: a sister who struggled to save small things from her brother's investigations, a woman powerless in the face of the men around her, a mother unable to defend her fetus from her partner's desire to abort it, a Canadian powerless in the face of the Americans who seem to be invading the wilderness regions of Canada. Gradually, though, the Surfacer abandons the illusion of her own innocence, recognizing that she is far from powerless and fully capable of hurting others. This marks an enormous step ahead since she spends most of the novel trying to submerge contradictory evidence—specifically, memories of the details of her abortion—in an effort to establish a case, in her own mind, to prove her powerlessness. However, her treatment of Joe, as well as her competent care of the others in the wilderness environment of the cabin, since she is the first one to set up camp, to fish, to put the vegetable garden in order, signal to the reader that she is not entirely powerless.

The Surfacer's inner journey is depicted in two different ways: first as a dive into the lake where, at the lake's bottom, she confronts her father's body and the memory of her aborted fetus; next as a descent into a kind of prelinguistic and primordial unity with nature and the "powers" that can be experienced through it. Both depictions resonate with well-known feminist texts of the twentieth century that describe women temporarily shedding the constraints imposed upon them by society and coming to terms with their own inner selves through a journey into the self that can be read either as a nervous breakdown or a period of rejuvenation and catharsis. Charlotte Perkins Gilman's short story "The Yellow Wallpaper" (1892) offers an example of a female narrator whose nervous breakdown and journey into madness lead to profound self-awareness as a woman held captive by her particular domestic situation and by society's gendered expectations. The passive role imposed on women is epitomized and represented in this story by the "rest cure" that the doctor imposes on the protagonist. Kate Chopin's *The Awakening* (1899) is another example, a novella describing Edna Pontellier's "awakening" to her unhappiness with married life and her increasing awareness about a distinction between her own and society's views of love, marriage, and sexuality more generally. In all three works, the central character's relationship to a man is contrasted with the established relationship of another couple. In all three, too, the central character's resistance is contrasted with another's woman's compliancy, even complacency. Both Atwood's and Chopin's novels are set near water, and both make use of images of diving and surfacing. Part of Atwood's point, one assumes, is that the Surfacer's situation in the 1970s is not so different from Edna's situation in the 1890s, despite the significant changes in women's history in the decades between these books. Other intertexts, or works that serve as useful points of comparison, include Doris Lessing's 1962 novel *The Golden Notebook*, which traces Anna's journey through nervous breakdown and toward a return to creativity, and Adrienne Rich's 1972 poem "Diving into the Wreck," which uses the image of a woman diving through a lake to describe her introspective look at her own psyche. Gwendolyn MacEwen's poem of the same year, "Dark Pines under Water" (*Shadow-Maker*) further emphasizes the introspective quality of the Canadian wilderness. *Surfacing* distinguishes itself from these other texts through the open-ended nature of its conclusion. We suspect, but cannot be sure, that the Surfacer will return to civilization. Consequently, Atwood leaves the Surfacer in the liberating landscape of the island, before she makes her decision and before she has had a chance to use language and thereby reenter society.

Another way of interpreting the Surfacer's behavior is that she, perhaps like her father before her, became "bushed," put temporary out of emotional and mental balance because of acute isolation. As such, the Surfacer we follow toward the end of the novel has grown much close to the wilderness landscape she inhabits, becoming more animal than socially civilized human. (Interpreted this way, of course, she is closer to the pioneer who approaches madness in Atwood's poem "Progressive Insanities of a Pioneer" than to the shaman.) This tension between an individual's role in society and in nature is one that appears frequently in Atwood's fiction. It receives its fullest treatment, however, in her poetry collection *The Journals of Susanna Moodie*. Here, Atwood traces the journey of pioneer gentlewoman Susanna Moodie (a real individual who is also referenced in Atwood's novel *Alias Grace* and in her play *The Servant Girl*) from nineteenth-century England to the Canadian bush. Atwood depicts Moodie as schizophrenic, arguing that she epitomizes the psychological disorder that afflicts Canada generally. Atwood's Surfacer anticipates Moodie in her journey from belonging to civilization to belonging to the wilderness. The difference is that whereas the Surfacer experiences these subsequently, Atwood's Moodie experiences them simultaneously.

The Surfacer's closing resolution to "refuse to be a victim" has further resonance in the Canadian context. In *Survival*, a popular introduction to Canadian literature published in the same year as *Surfacing* (1972), Atwood argues that Canadian literature is characterized by its depiction of a particular theme: the struggle for survival. She charts the development of this theme through four different victim positions, the first being "To deny the fact that you are a victim" (*Survival* 36) and the last involving the ability to be "a creative non-victim" because "external and/or internal causes of victimization have been removed"—which means "you are able to accept your own experience for what it is" (*Survival* 38–39). *Surfacing*'s depiction of its central character's struggle to survive a time of emotional upheaval, and her related struggle to survive the elements when she is left on the island alone with the various ghosts that haunt her, certainly proves to be a good illustration of Atwood's survival thesis. That is, if Atwood's *Survival* suggests that writers are "influenced by the country and cultural environment in which they work" (Jonas 63), then Atwood's *Surfacing* illustrates her point. As Atwood quite rightly points out, a novel's setting places constraints upon its form. The North is far more conducive to ghost stories, "[t]ales of obsession" or "hallucination," than to either "drawing-room comedies" or "epics" (Atwood, "Self-Discovery" 6).

HISTORICAL CONTEXT

Surfacing is set in the late 1960s and early 1970s, and the Surfacer's specifically feminist concerns can be seen against the backdrop of her times. Atwood's Marian MacAlpin of *The Edible Woman* charts her course amidst the options available to her as a young, single woman in the 1960s. Essentially, she decides whether to stay at work or to marry and settle down. One might assume that, with the introduction of the birth control pill (available in 1961 and legalized in 1969) and the sexual freedom it gave women, the Surfacer might find herself in a much stronger position as a woman of the 1970s. However, is she really any further ahead? Once divorced, the Surfacer is living with her partner, Joe. Yet he, like Peter in *The Edible Woman*, also pressures the protagonist to marry. Further, the Surfacer's crisis, prompted by the abortion of her first child, suggests that the liberation brought by the changing times has not liberated her from such age-old emotions as guilt. If the Surfacer finds herself any further ahead than her 1960s counterpart, it is a distance measured in inches rather than miles.

NARRATIVE STRUCTURE

There are at least two narratives developed in this novel: the search for clues about the Surfacer's missing father and the subsequent details of her response, and the surfacing of various ghosts from the past, including memories of an abortion and visions of her dead parents.

At one level, the first narrative is developed chronologically. We follow the Surfacer's search for her father as the clues appear and the evidence builds over the first week of her stay on the island. We know, for example, that she discovers his body while diving on the sixth day of her stay. Similarly, we follow her response to the crisis as she progressively rejects the outer signs of civilization over a period of days spent alone on the island. However, as James Harrison notes, the verb tenses shift between the present and past tenses in the three sections of the novel. Parts 1 and 3 are dominated by the present tense, when the Surfacer is absorbed in the details of surviving the particular challenges she encounters: mobilizing the search party and then surviving on her own. With the exception of the first four and the last three paragraphs (which are written in the present tense), part 3 is narrated in the past tense, when the Surfacer becomes absorbed in her own memories of childhood and marriage. Do these exceptions, as Harrison claims, suggest that one cannot separate one's present from one's past, since the latter always resurfaces?

The second narrative, involving the Surfacer's heightening intuition, is not developed chronologically. Rather, memories and visions appear as they are triggered by particular emotions or conversations. The logic of these visions is associative and symbolic. When her father appears to her, for example, he looks exactly like the drawing she made as a child, and he leaves only a trace of the Surfacer's own footprint. At one level, of course, this suggests that he is a figment of her imagination. It also illustrates that this second narrative is one of the movement of the Surfacer's mind. Time, in this narrative, is marked by the natural cycles of day and night, the appearance of the moon (which signals that time is right for her to conceive a child, for example). If time in the first narrative moves chronologically, then in the second narrative time is (loosely) cyclical.

NARRATIVE TECHNIQUE

Two narrative innovations are worth particular mention: Atwood's unreliable narrator and her use of poetry in a work of prose fiction.

Most of Atwood's first-person narratives are characterized by a particular kind of unreliable narrator: one who seems to be a wonderfully reliable observer of detail, but who is also remarkably unreliable in her interpretation of detail and events. Often called "flawed perceivers," these unreliable narrators appear in a number of well-known works of the twentieth century that aim to give readers a glimpse into a character's thoughts (especially those by such Modernist writers as Ford Madox Ford, Henry

James, James Joyce, and Virginia Woolf). William Faulkner's *The Sound and the Fury*, for example, opens with a section narrated by a mentally handicapped character. Consequently, readers see the character through what and how he or she sees. What characterizes Atwood's unreliable narrators, however, is the way they seem, at first glance, to be entirely reliable. Only after we are lured into trusting them do we start to see the signs of their duplicity. The Surfacer, whom we follow into a kind of nervous breakdown, is an excellent example.

The second narrative innovation is peculiar to this novel. At a certain moment in the Surfacer's breakdown, Atwood faces the dilemma of how to represent a woman who has abandoned language (as one of the trappings of civilization) in a novel that is written *in* language. She opts to slip from standardized prose and punctuation into lines of poetry, which themselves flow back to prose. Consequently, in chapter 25, just after the Surfacer has seen a vision of her father, the novel's lines shorten and become end-stopped, like the ragged-right-edged lines of poetry, before returning to the long lines of prose. In a section set apart from the rest of the chapter, the Surfacer pauses to notice a fish jump. But what at first appears to be a real fish jumping quickly become the "idea" of a fish jumping, then a "wooden fish," and later an "antlered fish thing" or "protective spirit," perhaps even a version of her own father, before returning to the original (187). Consequently, the narrative's movement from prose to poetry and back to prose follows the fish's own transformation from concrete reality and back again. One other example of the movement toward poetry occurs in chapter 24, as the Surfacer feels herself becoming transparent, a thing of nature, a "tree leaning" (181).

GENERIC CONVENTIONS

Atwood has described *Surfacing* as a ghost story in the vein of Henry James's *The Turn of the Screw* or *The Jolly Corner* ("Self-Discovery" 7). What distinguishes a Jamesian ghost story from others is the fact that James provides both ghosts in his stories and a logical explanation for why they might have appeared. Namely, the viewer is often in a particularly unstable or vulnerable frame of mind, so the ghost can be interpreted as an extension of the viewer's own unstable psyche. In the Surfacer's case, of course, she has undergone a tremendous upheaval, deprived herself of a balanced diet for some time before consuming some mushrooms of presumably questionable nature. Further, she has a tremendous desire to see her parents one last time to make amends for old wrongs. Consequently, readers are not entirely surprised when she stumbles upon her parents toward the end of the novel. What she perceives to be a powerful supernatural vision might also be interpreted, from the readers' point of view, as the logical function of her own state of mind.

Atwood has always been fascinated by the gothic genre, one that aims to evoke terror and makes use of supernatural elements, and *Surfacing* was neither her first nor her last ghost story. Her first unpublished novel, *Up in the Air So Blue*, was also in the gothic mode; and her next novel, *Lady Oracle*, can be read as a playful spoof on the gothic novel.

One gothic element in this novel is characteristic of the region in which the novel is set: the werewolves of traditional Quebec folk tales. Atwood was familiar with tales of the werewolf, or *loup garou*, having heard them as a child from her brother during the summers they spent in the wilderness with their entomologist father. To signal the relevance of the werewolf stories, the possibility of a wolf lurking in the heart of every civilized individual, Atwood gives the Surfacer a copy of *Quebec Folk Tales* to illustrate. Werewolf stories set out to chart the damage done by the werewolf and then follow the community in their search to locate and neutralize the danger. The werewolf in *Surfacing*, of course, proves difficult to locate. He first appears to be the Surfacer's father. Only later, as she moves closer to insanity or kinship with the natural world—or both—do we understand that it is the Surfacer herself. Highly problematic, the narrator turns out to be the source of her own gothic terror. This is a twist on the gothic tradition that occurs again in *Lady Oracle*.

A GENERIC READING

Genre is itself the French word for "kind" or "type." Genre criticism produces readings that examine the formal elements of the work and compare and contrast them with other works like it so as to establish a sense of the literary "kind" or "type." An important discussion of the role of genre in shaping a text and its readings appears in Alistair Fowler's book, *Kinds of Literature*. Genre critics explore the way a text's meaning is constructed and can be understood in relation to literary type. For example, a genre critic might note that a detective story with a female, rather than a male, protagonist goes against type. Such an observation might give rise to an interesting genre analysis, outlining the reasons behind the author's decision to cast a female sleuth in the lead role and discussing how that decision affects our reading of the novel as a detective fiction.

This reading compares *Surfacing* to a detective story, which it first appears to be. After all, the Surfacer's father has gone missing, and their arrival on the island marks the beginning of their search for him, as well as their search for clues as to his disappearance. Perhaps the most rigid genre of all, the detective story demands the plot to follow a particular trajectory: that of the quest. A quest is a search, but for a particular object or quality in which the searcher invests tremendous symbolic value. The Holy Grail, for example, is the object of the legendary quest of Sir Galahad of Arthurian legend. Sir Galahad, in this example, is the "quester." The equivalent of a detective in a detective fiction, the quester is the person charged with searching for the quest object.

Margaret Atwood, herself, identifies *Surfacing* not so much as a detective story but rather as a ghost story (Atwood, "Margaret Atwood" 20). One of the many ghosts haunting her novel is the quest narrative itself. It haunts the novel's critics as well. The first popular reading of *Surfacing* identified the narrative as archetypal, "dealing with a quest for rebirth and transformation" (Pratt 139). However, attention was subsequently focused on the parodic or exaggerated elements of the novel. Canadian literary critic Robert Lecker, for example, recognized that "the ending is shot through with irony" (186), and another Canadian literary critic, Eli Mandel, argued that "at the end, nothing is resolved" (169). Rather than being read as a quest narrative, *Surfacing* was now taken as a subversion of or an attack of that form. I want to pursue this second line of thought, merging it with a feminist reading of the novel. By identifying the duplicity in *Surfacing* as an explicitly feminist move on Atwood's part, I aim to explore and provide a reading of the novel's parody (an exaggeration intended to poke fun), even "unwriting," of quest narrative, as well as suggest some motives for it.

Critic Philip Kokotailo identifies a conflict in the criticism of *Surfacing* between the popular reading, in which the Surfacer is seen to emerge as a "newly integrated and realized self," and its antithesis, the denial of such a "central affirmation" in the novel (154–55). Of course, the latter parodic reading is a reaction against, and arises from, dissatisfaction with earlier critical attempts to impose a "quest for self" pattern on the Surfacer's journey. Clearly, the novel's ambiguous ending is inconsistent with any argument that posits the narrator's achieving a heightened sense of self, a clearer definition of her identity. Even proponents of the former "successful quest for self" reading find themselves forced to acknowledge that the conclusion of *Surfacing* is a radical departure from the quest pattern. When drawing a parallel between *Surfacing* and the detective novel, University of Toronto professor Russell Brown, for instance, admits that "the Surfacer discards her detective-like role and moves to the opposite extreme" ("In Search of Lost Causes" 10). Interestingly, in a later article, Brown suggests that Atwood has chosen to work with the popular genre of the detective novel specifically in order to "subvert" it, to "[turn] the mystery on its head." He sees Atwood at once "utilizing" and "rendering ironic" the genre's "forms, conventions, and clichés" (32). It is Robert Lecker, though, who has no reservations at all in making his case for Atwood's ironic intentions. He states bluntly that in *Surfacing* "there is a parody of all the conventions associated with 'search for identity' literature" (192).

Further, as Robert Lecker suggests, the novel's ambiguous conclusion is only the visible tip of a problematic iceberg. While the novel's lack of closure is cause for critical anxiety, it points to Atwood's even greater discomfort with the quest model and its closure. An inescapable problem with the "search for self" model, at least for *Surfacing*'s female author, is the male-dominated nature of quest narrative itself. In fact, I suggest that what has traditionally been termed the "search for self" or "quest for identity" would be more appropriately called the "conquest of identity." Rather than merely looking for his identity, the traditional quester has had to win it. This conquest takes the form of a rigid procedure that moves the protagonist from trials to a reward. The process, as Northrop Frye articulates it, involves three main stages: the "conflict," the "death struggle," and the "discovery" or "recognition of the hero, who has clearly proved himself to be a hero even if he does not survive the conflict" (187). Shakespeare's Coriolanus and Macbeth, for instance, receive their names as rewards for victories in battle. With their titles comes a knowledge of themselves in relation to others in the society and, consequently, a certain sense of closure. Most notably, the pursuit as well as the attainment of title is a male endeavor. It is not that women do not exist in these quest narratives. Female protagonists in search of their identities are admitted in the gothic romance tradition, but they win only the right to a man's name, to an identity in relation to a superior other, and can only be as powerful as their subordinate position allows. In short, females are allowed to be heroines but not heroes.

Surfacing's relation to this "conquest of identity" model is one of stark contrast: a mirror reflection. In fact, the calculated inversion of conquest provides for a pattern so reminiscent of the three-part discovery that critics, as I mentioned earlier, have mistaken the novel for the very identity quest narrative it parodies (Pratt, Campbell). *Surfacing*, that is, seems to be an "unwriting" of the "conquest of identity," or a calculated subversion of it. Within the novel, the Surfacer not only resents "Americans"—an umbrella term that comes to represent colonialists, imperialists, and males—but the novel is itself an attack on imperialism and its tool, the quest narrative.

To be sure, in the Surfacer's quest, Atwood counters each characteristic of the "conquest of identity," highlighting the signposts of her "unconquering." First, and most obviously, the protagonist valorizes victims rather than victors. In her eyes, to be a hero is to be a "killer," to be guilty. Only victims are innocent. And although she has sanctioned the killing of others—leeches, fish, her own fetus—that part of herself is another ghost that haunts her. It reminds her that she must not only "refuse to be a victim" (191) but also refuse to be a killer. She must act against the dictates of a society that institutionalizes murder and calls it by such names as hunting, abortion, and war. That is, while the traditional quest hero fights battles, Atwood's Surfacer fights against them. Second, although the Surfacer survives her plunge into the real and metaphorical lake, she receives no name as a reward. Neither king nor witch hails her by a new title. She neither marries to take on her husband's name nor dies to be memorialized in words. Further, an even greater subversion of the "quest for identity" than Atwood's refusal to name her narrator is the Surfacer's own refusal to identify herself. By telling us "I no longer have a name" (168), the Surfacer relinquishes her right even to the name that Atwood already withhold from us. Third, rather than confirming the Surfacer's identity in relation to others in the society around her, her search involves a questioning of those relations and the alienation that questioning aggravates. As the Surfacer remains isolated on the island at the end of the novel, even her physical return to society is questionable. That tentative ending is a fourth contrast to the "conquest" format and the closure it involves. At the end, nothing has been "clearly proved," and she may not live happily ever after. That the protagonist is female and her pregnancy is the catalyst for resolution are the final differences. The vehicle for resolution in this female "unwriting" of the conquest form is life and not death, silence rather than the closure of naming.

Specifically what is it about the quest narrative that provokes such an attack from Atwood? Suggestions about her "interest in the conventions of romance, particularly as they emerge in Gothic literature" (Lecker 192), or her "obsessive concern with mirror and reflection" (Mandel 174) seem inadequate to explain such a focused and pointed response. Robert Lecker comments that *Surfacing* is a parody because the quest motif "must itself be seen as a sham in a culture where rituals have lost their potency" (194).

Although there is undeniably a parodic inversion of the "search for self," it is impossible to locate the source in the impotence of ritual. Rather than losing their power, rituals have changed. They may not be as obvious as the killing of a Fisher King (what James Frazer in *The Golden Bough* cites as the central motif of Western literature), but the Surfacer recognizes ritual and pattern in her media-filled world nonetheless. She knows, for instance, that communication itself has become ritualized. When Anna gives advice on marriage, her tone of voice changes. "People's voices go radio when they give advice," the narrator tells us (47). David's voice is often stylized, in his "skits" with Anna (44) or in his imitations of Woody Woodpecker, Goofy, or other cartoon characters. Actually, men in Surfacing often communicate through maxims, using borrowed phrases instead of relying on their natural voice. The Surfacer's father makes epigrams (9), David uses one-liners, her childhood friend's father says grace in the form of a comic couplet (56), and even Joe makes use of the occasional cliché (124).

But ritual has not only been modernized, transformed by mass media, it also appears to have changed because it is seen from a female perspective. As readers, we are more used to hearing the knight's story, a tale about the quest he performs and the trials he faces for his waiting maiden; but Atwood and her narrator are more concerned with that maiden's story. The Surfacer wonders about what the fairy tales did *not* reveal, what the characters ate or "whether their towers and dungeons had bathrooms" (54). In her own life, for example, the Surfacer is acutely aware of the female side of the rituals of courtship and lovemaking. She understands, for instance that makeup is important enough to Anna that her daily routine includes waking early to preen herself before the mirror. In the summer, that routine includes tanning outdoors, Anna's "sun rituals" (100). Whether David even knows about the ritual performed for his benefit is questionable: he may perceive the finished product, a tanned Anna with immaculate makeup, as natural.

In fact, men seem to be distanced from women in Surfacing, a function of their language and their attitude. All women of a certain age in the Quebecois community, the Surfacer notices, are called "madame." That is, none of the women seem to have individual names (27). Although David propositions the Surfacer, initiating some closer individual contact, his motives are distinctly impersonal. Approaching the Surfacer is no more than a strategic maneuver in the power play she calls David's "geometrical sex" (152). The Surfacer understands that she is a pawn to be toppled in the game David is playing with his wife, Anna. She understands her role as the "other woman" in the modern-day ritual.

Instead, Atwood attacks the quest motif because of its inappropriateness for a female author and a female protagonist. Especially in her antigothic novel, *Lady Oracle*, Atwood shows herself to be acutely aware of the confining nature of narrative and the "perils of gothic thinking" (qtd. in Struthers 23), at least for women. Joan Foster fights against the constraints of the gothic romance as its pattern encroaches on her own life. She sees herself as an escape artist, "entering the embrace of bondage, slithering out again" (*Lady Oracle* 367). Writing out of a feminist tradition, her project is one of "ridding herself of mythologies" (Brown, "Atwood's Sacred Wells" 32), "un-naming," "demythologizing," and "uninventing" the world (Kroetsch "Unhiding" 43).

But the problematic task of "unwriting" cannot be completed in one antagonistic slash of the pen. The very characteristics that make the conquest narrative confining also contribute to its long-standing popularity: a logical sequence of events that lead to closure. For a writer whose task involves communicating to an audience trained to read linear narrative, there are two courses of action: to undermine the plot structure or the language in which it is expressed. To simultaneously wage war on both fronts would only weaken the offensive. Atwood's recognition of this dilemma is evident when she chooses that her narrator continue to communicate despite her evident suspicion of language. Rosemary Sullivan calls Atwood to task on this very decision. "Atwood's language fails her," Sullivan writes. "Even in moments of intense mystical perception, her language is the language of logic. She does not experiment with language, she does not go far enough" (40). But, here, I argue that the thrust of Atwood's attack is articulated through the narrative structure and not through the language of the novel; clarity of expression is too valuable a weapon to sacrifice.

What is the narrative alternative to conquest? Atwood's answer is what Rachel Blau du Plessis has since called "reparenting." Instead of a finite search for her father, the Surfacer returns to "extend, reveal and elaborate" (93) her parents' thwarted task. Like her father, she finds the drawings and their power. But rather than "capturing" the power with a camera, she is able to nurture and release that power through the pregnancy her mother inspires. The father's disappearance, then, is little more than an excuse to justify her returning to the island: a notion that would explain why the novel does not end when the Surfacer solves the mystery.

Why does the Surfacer idealize her mother to such an extent? To be sure this idealization serves two purposes in that it provides the narrator with a figure who is both a mythical source of healing power and a human role model. Through becoming a mother in her own right, the narrator is able to approach that power and appropriate it as her own. "The only place left for me," says the Surfacer, "is that of my mother" (58). She can be at once a mother and be mothered, a desire not so inconsistent as it sounds. As Jane Flax notes, "Women often admit that one motive for becoming a mother is to regain a sense of being mothered themselves" (174). The Surfacer's need for security is particularly evident in her paradoxical nostalgia for the "peaceful" time of her wartime childhood and the regression to childhood that she experiences. As she tries to prevent herself from running back from the outhouse, for instance, she tells herself, "stop it, I'm old enough. I'm old" (173). Further, her second pregnancy is a chance to become a good mother rather than a failed one. If, as Roberta Rubenstein suggests, "it is the narrator's failure of maternity that exacerbates her self-alienation" (391), then successfully becoming a mother would restore her health and would allow for her reintegration into society.

But the Surfacer's appeal to an idealized childhood and to an explicitly archetypal mother figure is only temporary. She eventually recognizes that her parents were mortal and that their godlike perfection was something she herself had wished upon them. She says her parents "dwindle, grow, become what they were, human. Something I never gave them credit for; but their totalitarian innocence was my own" (189–90). In a pivotal scene, she first seems to establish the fact that her parents did appear before her because of the footprints they leave behind, but she later understands that the prints are her own (187). There is "no total salvation," she realizes. That is, she learns that archetypal salvation, like religion, like the quest story, is unreal. And all she has is reality.

I suggest, then, that the implicit and alternative quest is for the mother as much as the father. And when the Surfacer finds them, both her parents lead her to understand that ultimate solutions are fictional, and by implication, inadequate. Rather than reaching a completion of quest, then, the Surfacer finally sees the need to escape from the realm of story. Her eventual indecision characterizes Atwood's unwriting of ending as well as the Surfacer's initial and tentative steps toward freedom. The question of what the Surfacer will do next must remain unanswered; Atwood's process of "unwriting conquest" involves nurturing alternatives rather than eliminating them.

Of course, Margaret Atwood's later heroines will voice their distrust of story more openly, and Atwood's subversion of narrative models will be more explicit. But if one overlooks the parodic elements in *Surfacing,* then one also ignores many of the novel's subtle implications and their significance to the development of Atwood's feminist aesthetic.

5

Lady Oracle
(1976)

Atwood's two earliest published novels introduce thematic concerns that remain with her throughout her career: the protection of individual rights (including women's rights) and of the wilderness. Atwood's third novel, *Lady Oracle*, focuses on the female artist figure, a character introduced in *Surfacing* and found at the heart of most of Atwood's subsequent novels. By allowing the artist of *Lady Oracle*, a writer, to narrate this novel, Atwood not only puts the spotlight on her dilemma as inheritor of a distinctly male-dominated artistic tradition, but also on her strategies for resolving her concerns. As such, *Lady Oracle* introduces a third, and central, and recurring theme of Atwood's work: writing. It also reveals a wide range of strategies that a contemporary female feminist writer might adopt to challenge the male-centered literary tradition. *Lady Oracle* itself, as well as many of the books written by the artist figure within it, trouble conventional expectations of plot, setting, and character. Atwood's subsequent novels will do this as well, as the next three chapters reveal. However, whereas Atwood's other novels tend to challenge character, setting, *or* plot, *Lady Oracle*'s endearing artist figure takes aim at all three, and all at once.

PLOT DEVELOPMENT

Any discussion of plot development here must be prefaced by a comment about the importance of humor in the novel. *Lady Oracle*, like *The*

Edible Woman, is hilariously funny. Both spoofs (*Lady Oracle* on the gothic novel and *The Edible Woman* on the feminist political tract), these novels tickle readers' funny bones while engaging their social consciences.

The novel opens with the central character's admission that, although she had planned her (fake) death carefully, her life was not so tightly controlled. It quickly becomes clear that Joan Foster, the central character who narrates the novel, is larger than life in who she is and what she does. In the first of many mirror images in this novel, Joan explains that her life "ballooned and festooned" like the frame of an ornate baroque mirror (3). Even her tears are dramatically overdone. She sobs gracelessly about being alone in Terremoto, Italy, where she had vacationed with her husband, Arthur, only the year before. She also cries about *being* so graceless in her sobbing.

Joan is in concealment, trying to shed the signs of her former life yet still torn by a longing for it. She cuts her distinctive waist-length hair and later dyes it, and puts her clothes in a garbage bag in a crack in the house's foundation. Although she is friendly with her landlord, Mr. Vitrioni, she is careful not to give away too much information about herself. Pleased that she has pulled off the caper so well, she opens a bottle of Cinzano to celebrate the end of her old life and the beginning of her new one. However, the caper's success is muted by Joan's thoughts of her husband, Arthur. She doesn't contact him, but does remember to send the coded postcard to Sam indicating that she has escaped successfully.

Realizing she is short of cash, Joan concludes that she will have to begin writing a new novel. Chapter 4, then, reveals Joan's secret identity as a writer of "costume gothics," that is, gothic romances of the dime-store variety. The one she is working on now is called *Stalked by Love*, a title that includes the notions of both love (central to romance) and terror (central to gothic). We are introduced to the central characters of Joan's novel: Redmond, the hero; Felicia, his evil wife; and Charlotte, who is both innocent and beautiful. Joan defends this kind of literature on the grounds that it provides women with a form of escape. Joan, given her current situation, seems to believe in a woman's need to escape. After all, she seems justified in feeling threatened. For example, the novel's first eight pages were stolen by Fraser Buchanan, but, as insurance, she managed to take his journal.

As well as being an escape artist, Joan seems to be skilled in the art of concealment. She tells Arthur little of her childhood, for example, the details of which are given to readers in part 2, or chapters 5 through 11. These read like the reminiscences of a comedian, shaped by a childhood that is so outrageously traumatic that it becomes almost funny. Her mother had called her Joan, after the movie star Joan Crawford. However, Joan's own public performances are not as positive as her mother obviously hoped. Joan recalls an early ballet performance where, because of her large size, the teacher Miss Flegg forced her to don a moth costume rather than the coveted butterfly costume for the butterfly dance. The audience response was overwhelmingly positive and the scene a great success, but it was at the large young Joan's expense.

This scene proved pivotal to Joan's understanding that thin women and fat women are treated entirely differently. Joan, a very fat little girl, was not treated well. In chapter 6, she remembers her time in Brownies. Her mother had joined her to a chapter in a wealthier neighborhood, so she was forced to walk quite a distance in the company of three other girls: Marlene, Lynne, and Elizabeth. The walk itself takes them over treacherous terrain, over the deep ravine, and past the "daffodil man" (a flasher who moves the daffodils to expose his genitals). The three little girls torment Joan, who proves to be an easy target. The week after seeing the daffodil man, they tie Joan up and leave her in the ravine. Ironically, the man who rescues her may indeed be the daffodil man himself. From this lesson, Joan understands that it is often difficult to tell bad men from good ones.

When it comes to women, however, Joan seems to be more certain. Her mother is unambiguously frightening. In chapter 7, Joan recalls two dreams she used to have about her mother. In both of them, she seems to be monstrous. The first involves Joan falling off a bridge into the ravine and her mother ignoring her. The second describes the way her mother seems to have three heads as Joan watches her reflection in the three-way makeup mirror. Clearly Joan's excessive eating is vengeful, prompted perhaps by her desire to make herself visible to her ever-disappointed mother or to resist her mother's obvious desire to have a thin and beautiful daughter. The mother treats her husband with no greater respect. At one dinner, she regales guests with stories of how her anesthetist husband murdered people during the war.

Joan finds a surrogate mother in the wonderful Aunt Lou, who embodies everything that her mother is not. Aunt Lou, for example, is divorced. Her husband was a gambler, and she now goes out with a married man, the accountant Robert. As the head of public relations at a company that manufactures feminine-hygiene products, Lou is not the kind of person Joan's mother invites to dinner. Aunt Lou takes Joan to movies, where she first sees the film of *The Red Shoes*, and to "the Ex," a large fair held in

Toronto each year. Sensitive to Joan, she refuses to allow her into the Freak Tent where the Fat Lady presides.

Rather than tell Arthur about her obese youth, Joan tells him the girl in the picture with Aunt Lou is her Aunt Deirdre, whom she describes as a "bitch." The narrative then explores whether Joan, underneath it all, really was a "bitch" in her adolescent years. Although never invited to parties, she befriended the popular girls and listened carefully to their romantic plights. These, of course, become raw material for Joan's later costume gothics. Further, Joan realizes, those same girls, some of whom have married and had children too early, have become her readers. In chapter 9, Joan reflects on her first two "sexual" experiences. The first occurs when a thwarted adolescent male buries his face in her large stomach. The second takes the form of a marriage proposal from an immigrant man impressed by Joan's heft, which signals her potential for strong motherhood, who proposes at the Bite-A-Bit restaurant where she works.

Chapters 1 through 9 focus on Joan's physical and emotional development, but chapter 10 examines her spiritual development. The subject is prompted by a dinner invitation from Aunt Lou, who invites Joan to meet Robert and to go to the spiritualist church. At first, Joan is somewhat skeptical of the spiritual leader, Leda Sprott, but becomes more intrigued when she's told she has "great powers" and should try the automatic-writing class. These powers help Joan to see her mother's spirit one night (the first of many ghostly appearances in this book), a vision that is not entirely pleasant because Joan's mother is not yet dead. Joan is told that it must be her mother's astral body. Moreover, the automatic writing proves equally unpleasant. When trying it one night, Joan leans into the candle by mistake and sets her hair on fire.

In the next chapter, Joan is indeed proven to have a certain sixth sense. At the very moment Joan is shot in the bottom by an overly zealous archer (she is working a booth at the Sportsman's Show at the Ex), Aunt Lou dies of a heart attack. In her will, she leaves Joan $2,000 on the condition that she loses 100 pounds. This bequest, together with Joan's frame of mind after Lou's death (when she develops blood poisoning from the arrow and, examining her thigh closely one day, feels disgust at her size and shape), and her mother's increasing hysteria (she actually stabs Joan with a knife in the heat of an argument), prompts Joan to leave home and move on to the next stage of her life.

Part 3 outlines this next stage, when Joan sheds the requisite number of pounds and begins her life as an author of costume gothics. Chapter 12, however, takes us momentarily back to the novel's present, where Joan buys a used typewriter in Terremoto and takes up the novel, *Stalked by Love*, so as to access some ready cash. The chapter opens with a few pages of the novel itself, signaled by italics. Here Charlotte (hired as a jeweler by Redmond and his wife, Felicia) watches Felicia in intimate conversation with a lover and then turns to find Redmond close beside her. She is clearly uncomfortable with his advances, improper under the circumstances. She is even more troubled when, upon returning to her room, she finds all her clothes slashed.

The narrative returns to Joan, as she prepares for her departure from Toronto. Until she can lose enough weight, she lives in a hotel in Toronto and occupies herself with museum visits and bus trips. But as soon as she can, she claims her inheritance and buys a plane ticket to England. While she finds the country less exciting than she had expected, she finds the possibilities now available to her, as a thin and attractive woman, positively exhilarating. Quite by accident, she meets the Polish Count as she falls getting off a double-decker bus. He immediately takes her under his wing, and when she is kicked out of her damp, undesirable rooming house because her landlord catches him bandaging her ankle, she moves in with him. She sleeps with him, an event he takes lightly, thinking that she has had prior experience. Joan later tells Arthur her first time was with a summer camp counselor in her adolescence.

While exploring the apartment, Joan finds a revolver and a curious selection of nurse books. When she asks him about the books, he explains that they are his, written under the pseudonym Mavis Quilp. Soon, she begins writing costume gothics under the pen name Louisa K. Delacourt. Very soon, short of money, Joan becomes more prolific than Paul (the real name of the Polish Count), and he becomes resentful.

When Joan walks through Hyde Park in London one day, envisioning an escape scene in her most recent novel, she is startled by a hand on her arm: Arthur's. She falls for him almost immediately, and they go out to a pub. She tries to ingratiate herself by reading Bertrand Russell, whom she later parodies in her novel. Her situation with Paul goes from bad to worse, and she decides to leave him for Arthur. She shows up at Arthur's door, claiming her landlord evicted her for her political leanings. Things at his apartment are difficult because of his two roommates, one of whom pawns her typewriter, making it impossible for her to type *Escape from Love* and hence earn the money she sorely needs.

Chapter 16 ends with the appearance, in Arthur's apartment, of her mother's ghost. This time, her mother really has died, as she finds out via telegram after the ghostly vision. She spends two days in the library fin-

dynamite. Instead of targeting the peace bridge, she and the Royal Porcupine explode the dynamite on a patch of land in the park. Everyone is delighted when it obtains press coverage.

Chapter 27 outlines Joan's growing anxieties about the increasingly threatening situation around her. There are threatening phone calls and notes, as well as dead animals left on her doorstep. Worse, perhaps, she begins to see apparitions of the Fat Lady, who appears on the television screen, in a pink outfit. Who or what is the source of such threats is unclear. However, a number of possibilities emerge. One is Paul, who appears out of the blue, ostensibly to rescue Joan from Arthur. Another is Fraser Buchanan, whom Joan finds rifling through her drawers as she emerges from the bathtub one day. Rather than phone the police, she goes out for drinks with him. Those drinks, and a bit of initiative on Joan's part, make it possible for her to steal his little black book, thereby gaining the upper hand in their negotiation.

However, by chapter 28, Joan has resolved to mastermind her escape from the increasingly maze-like series of identities she has created for herself. Explaining that the dynamite has been found, she solicits the help of Sam and Marlene, but decides that Arthur should know nothing of the plan. Joan buys a ticket to Rome, rents a car, and goes sailing with Sam and Marlene. At the planned moment, she falls of the boat, floats on shore and safely makes her way to the airport. With the exception of Sam and Marlene, everyone thinks she has drowned.

If part 4 ends with Joan's "death," part 5 traces the ripples caused by it. Sam sends Joan a package containing a press clipping about her presumed suicide. Through her death, she has gained a new kind of celebrity, similar to that of a Sylvia Plath or Anne Sexton, both of whom committed suicide at a young age. Despite some sense of longing to return to her former life, Joan realizes that she can never really go back.

She plans the ending for *Stalked by Love:* Felicia would have to die, and Charlotte would either have a final confrontation with Redmond, possibly hitting him over the head with a sharp object (an event that foreshadows the ending of Atwood's *Lady Oracle* itself), or being rescued by Redmond. In either scenario, Redmond would reveal his true love for Charlotte, and she would recognize hers for him. The only problem is that Joan feels a desire to make Felicia more sympathetic, not to kill her off. Frustrated, Joan takes a break, only to confront yet another apparition of the Fat Lady, this time growing out of the clothes she had hidden in the house's foundation.

The Fat Lady seems to haunt Joan's novel as well. In the continuation,

Felicia drowns only to reappear, in fatter form, to take revenge on Redmond. Clearly Joan's life and fiction are no longer separate entities. Indeed, Joan adopts the pose of the threatened heroine when Mr. Vitrioni, the landlord, explains that the community is curious about why she hid her clothes, cut her hair, and always wears dark glasses. He explains, too, that there is a man looking for her. She tells him that she is extremely wealthy and is hiding from someone who is trying to kill her. He seems to believe her and offers to help. She refuses, planning to escape again, as she has done so many times before. That her car is out of gas, however, presents a problem. (Has the tank been siphoned?) So, temporarily stymied, she goes to bed, only to be threatened from another source: the ghost of her mother, which appears for the third time in this novel.

As Joan's situation builds to a crescendo, so too does her novel. *Stalked by Love* comes to the moment when Charlotte must enter the maze and, presumably, confront Felicia at its center. In a symbolic sense, Joan also enters a maze when she goes into the village to find the latest package from Sam containing news items about the arrest of Sam and Marlene, both suspected of involvement in a terrorist plot that resulted in Joan's death. Here, of course, the maze involves the labyrinthine deception that she has constructed around herself. Feeling guilty about Sam and Marlene, Joan notices Mr. Vitrioni with the man who is looking for her. However, she cannot identify him.

Joan retreats to her apartment and waits. As she sits crouched, gripping a Cinzano bottle (presumably the same one she had used to toast her new life), she pictures her novel once again. This time, Felicia (rather than Charlotte) has entered the maze and at its center she finds four women: two with long red hair like Joan's, another who resembles Aunt Lou, and the Fat Lady. All are, of course, versions of Joan, and all claim to be Lady Redmond. At this moment, Joan's life and her novel have merged entirely. Redmond appears to take her away, but she refuses. His face then changes features, cycling through the various men of Joan's life. At this moment, Joan hears a noise in her apartment and prepares to strike.

While chapter 36 leaves us in suspense, chapter 37 begins after the man has recovered consciousness. It reads like a confession from Joan. She hadn't really meant to hit him with the bottle so hard that he needed stitches. He's really, on second thought, a "nice man." Though she's not a tidy person, Joan vows to go home and straighten out all the mess she's left behind. But in the meantime, she visits this individual, whose identity remains ambiguous, in the hospital.

CHARACTER DEVELOPMENT

Why, Joan wonders in chapter 1, can't she be like the graceful heroines of novels? By this, she seems to mean like the heroine of gothic romances and, more particularly, of costume gothics. The answer is that Joan is not so much a heroine as she is the parody of one, so exaggerated as to poke fun at and expose the flat and two-dimensional nature of literary heroines who act predictably. Indeed, Joan's multifaceted personality is so exaggerated that she exposes the predictability of even the most rounded and three-dimensional of literary heroines. Most obviously, rather than being one single character, Joan plays the role of at least four different individuals: Joan Foster, wife of Arthur; Joan Foster, author of *Lady Oracle*; Aunt Deidre, the name she gives her obese younger self; and Louisa K. Delacourt, author of costume gothic. Further, the Fat Lady who appears like a ghostly apparition throughout the novel is clearly a project of Joan's psyche. She is the incarnation of Joan's anxieties about her childhood and the excessiveness of her personality. At one point in the novel, Joan's mother asks her just who does she think she is? The question has an edge to it and implies that Joan is getting too presumptuous, too big for her boots. At the time, Joan offers her mother no answers. But the novel details Joan's multiple answers to the question as she eats herself into existence and then imagines herself into multiple existences. As such, Joan also embodies Atwood's response or challenge to the rigid conventions of literary characterization. Atwood, in *Lady Oracle*, proves that literary characters do not have to be consistent or unified to be engaging.

Joan's name is appropriate for at least two reasons (and Joan Crawford fans might be able to come up with others). Most obviously, Joan Foster "fosters" a number of different identities for herself, just as she "fosters" different stories about herself. As well, for readers who, like Atwood, enjoy the fiction of Canadian writer Lucy Maud Montgomery, author of the popular series *Anne of Green Gables*, the name might "foster" a different comparison. "*John* Foster" is the name of a character in Maud Montgomery's novel *Blue Castle*, about the young Valancy Stirling's thwarted, and then later realized, dreams of romance. As Terri Zurbrigg explains, when the world seems to press down too hard upon her, she finds solace in "an ongoing fantasy about a Blue Castle in Spain in which she takes various lovers whose appearances change and evolve according to her tastes in men and the books of John Foster" (letter to author). John Foster is clearly, like Joan-alias–Louisa K. Delacourt and Mavis Quilp, an author of escapist fiction. Valancy knows that he is a Canadian writer and is pretty sure that John Foster is a "nom de plume." But what really intrigues her about

Foster's writing is "some tantalizing lure of a mystery never revealed— some hint of a giant secret just a little further on" (13).

Part of the point of the novel is that Joan is the most rounded of possible characters. She is not only developed, but also *over*developed. Compared with Joan, then, the other female characters seem very flat and two-dimensional. Joan's mother, for example, is one of the gorgons of Atwood's novels, a woman who is so unequivocally nasty as to be almost mythic in proportion. Although Winifred Griffen of *The Blind Assassin* is her equal in nastiness, Aunt Muriel, the gorgon of *Life before Man*, seems to win a bit of sympathy as she lies in her hospital bed. Frustrated in her role as a housewife and in her efforts to transform Joan into a paragon of beauty and grace, Joan's mother shows little sympathy for either Joan or her father. Aunt Lou, though far more sympathetic and great fun, is also a flat or undeveloped character. If Joan's mother is described in a clearly negative light, then her Aunt Lou is described in a purely positive one. As such, these two mother figures are character foils for one another. Other secondary female characters remain relatively consistent. The adult Marlene, for example, is not so different from her younger self. Even Leda Sprott, who does assume a different name and guise as reverend, ultimately plays the same role as she had in her former incarnation: that of the spiritual advisor–cum–con artist.

True to the gothic tradition, in which male characters are threatening because ambiguous, the men in Atwood's novel have a double identity. Joan's father, for example, was, as her mother describes him at her dinner party, a murderer during the war, but now works as an anesthetist and saver of lives. The daffodil man in the park is both the flasher who terrifies the young Brownies and, possibly, the man who rescues Joan when the Brownies tie her up and leave her in the ravine. Paul the Polish Count leads a secret life as Mavis Quilp, author of costume gothics, especially romance novels featuring nurses. As well as being the Byronic hero that Joan appreciates, the Royal Porcupine is also the prosaic Chuck Brewer. Even Arthur is far more than Joan's husband. At the very least, he is a political activist and possibly, after discovering clues about her various affairs, he even perpetrates the various threats to Joan, including the phone calls, notes, and dead animals. Finally, Fraser Buchanan, the journalist who searches Joan's apartment, may, although we're not entirely sure, be the "nice" man who intrudes upon her apartment in Italy. Only the character of Mr. Vitrioni, who is a very marginal character in the drama, seems entirely consistent and one-dimensional. Even he, however, may have questionable motives, a notion that becomes apparent toward the end of the novel when Joan sees him in the company of the journalist who is pursuing her.

NARRATIVE STRUCTURE

If Joan's larger-than-life personality embodies Atwood's challenge to the conventions of literary characterization, then the novel's inverted plot illustrates her challenge to the conventions of linear realism. When a plot is linear, it means that the story moves from start to end in a logical and predictable pattern. However, *Lady Oracle* is anything but predictable. For instance, it begins with an ending: the opening scene actually describes a death (Joan's faked suicide), and is spoken by the individual who has died. (As such, it provides a similar effect to Atwood's poem "This Is a Photograph of Me" [*The Circle Game*], in which the speaker identifies him or herself as being underwater, drowned.) The novel proceeds to circle around the circumstances behind and effects of this faked suicide until, in the novel's final chapter, it returns to the very point at which it began. In other words, the novel ends at its beginning. Far from being a linear narrative that moves from point *a* to point *b*, then, it becomes a circular narrative. Joan recognizes this deficiency when, in the last chapter, she bemoans the lack of a "lesson" in her story, the usual endpoint of a linear or journey narrative.

The novel is unpredictable in a different way as well, one that directly challenges the conventions of realism. After all, realist narratives are meant to convey the illusion that they are representations of lived experience. However, *Lady Oracle* contains a number of rather unsettling supernatural occurrences. Take the example of Joan's mother, whose astral body appears at least three times. Whereas the ghostly experiences of *Surfacing* can be explained by the Surfacer's frame of mind, there is little about Joan that might serve as a rational explanation for these visions. The Fat Lady's appearances function in a similar way.

Are these ghost-like figures a suggestion that Joan's habit of seeing her life in terms of fiction has just gone too far? Even if this is the case, Atwood's readers find themselves sharing the illusion and, in doing so, gaining a new perspective on realist fiction. Perhaps, then, they are a suggestion that the linear plot, which moves systematically from beginning to end and describes characters who are stable and predictable, is just not suitable for a woman like Joan. Perhaps, to take it one step further, *Lady Oracle* suggests that the linear plot may be inadequate.

If Joan's life "scrolls and festoons" like the frame of a baroque mirror, so too does the narrative of her life that is Atwood's *Lady Oracle* (3). This novel is metafictional, a fiction about fiction. Contained within Atwood's novel, *Lady Oracle,* are a series of other novels, with various descriptions of the circumstances in which they are written and read.

Joan Foster herself writes a book of poetry called *Lady Oracle,* which is well received by audiences, read as a combination of Kahil Gibran and Rod McKuen by her publishers, and as a *roman à clef* (a work of fiction presenting actual persons or events) about her marriage by Arthur. As readers, we have the advantage of overhearing all these different readings of Joan's book and also of hearing the circumstances of its production, prompted by the word "bow," which comes to Joan during a session of automatic writing. As well, we can see the trace of another influence beside whatever is behind the mirror: Tennyson's ballad "The Lady of Shalott," which Joan had studied in high school. This additional piece to the interpretive puzzle allows us to recognize the source of Joan's inspiration for her book *Lady Oracle.* It also foreshadows the outcome of its publication for Joan. More specifically, the poem is about an artist figure, a woman who weaves what she sees in her mirror, placed so as to catch the images of those passing by on the river behind her. The curse of the Lady of Shalott is the curse of all artists: she is doomed to experience life only indirectly, to gaze upon it only through the mirror. However, when she sees a handsome man go by, she decides to risk the curse and, as she does so, the mirror that has showcased the world for her cracks dramatically. Anticipating the worst, she paints her name on a boat and sails down the river to meet her fate. But by the time she approaches the man she had seen, she is dead and has become the heroine of the narrative rather than its safely removed author.

Joan, too, will invoke this curse during the moments when she becomes gothic heroine rather than writer of gothic fiction. Her first faked death is, of course, a comic version of the Lady of Shalott's dramatic gesture: both women artists have taken the plunge toward escape. Whereas Tennyson's heroine dies, however, Atwood's Joan resurfaces in Terremoto. Does Joan survive because her mirror never cracks entirely? After all, while in Italy, she continues to write her costume gothics and to maintain a separation between life and art. Only at the very end of the novel, as the intruder becomes her confessor, does the mirror crack entirely. But Atwood's novel ends where the Lady of Shalott's journey begins. We can only guess what will be the outcome of Atwood's narrative.

THEMATIC DEVELOPMENT

Of the various themes in this novel, two are of particular importance: the desire for escape and the realization that escape is impossible.

The desire for escape is illustrated by Joan's Houdiniesque habit of slipping sideways out of her life, into either the books she is writing or the stories she is telling. The heroines of her costume gothics are also characterized by their desire to escape, of course. So, too, are a number of Atwood's heroines who serve as interesting prototypes of Joan. The difference between Atwood's heroines and those of Joan's costume gothics, however, is that they are not only prisoners in a kind of trap; they also invent and maintain the trap. These include Joan herself, as well as the speakers in Atwood's poem "This Is a Photograph of Me" and "Siren Song."

One can trace a number of attempted escapes in *Lady Oracle:* from the various pseudonyms Joan adopts to the faked suicide. Ultimately, however, Joan never pulls them off. The reporter, Fraser Buchanan, was clearly onto her before she faked her death; and the reporter who follows her to Italy has clearly cottoned on to that as well. In botching her planned escapes, Joan seems to differ from any of the tragic female artist figures with whom we might implicitly associate her, but especially from the sacrificial female artist with whom the novel associates her: Tennyson's Lady of Shalott. Joan, to put it bluntly, blunders the escape and stays very much alive. Unlike the frail heroines of gothic, Joan is larger than life, and finds it very hard to stay silent and invisible.

Part of the problem is that she is not a gothic heroine at all (in the way that the Lady of Shalott proved herself capable of being). Joan is an artist and, as such, is better compared to the heroine of Joan's favorite film, *The Red Shoes* with Moira Shearer, which she watches at least four times in chapter 8. Like Joan, the principal character, a ballerina named Victoria, has red hair. Also like Joan, try as she might, Victoria cannot escape the fact that she is an artist. Although she opts for marriage to the orchestra conductor over a career as a ballerina (choosing both is not a possibility in this film), she eventually finds herself drawn back to her red shoes. The film ends when Victoria puts them on and they dance her, or she dances with them, toward the train tracks and the oncoming train. Joan's own path is somewhat similar. She, too, opts for marriage at first. But it doesn't take long before she feels the need to go back to writing. Realizing the parallel to Moira Shearer in the film, as well as to the Little Mermaid in the Hans Christian Anderson fairy tale, she rationalizes her decision by explaining to herself that Victoria's mistake was going public with her art. By contrast, she danced "behind closed doors" (218). The problem, however, is that she does not stick to her resolve. Her next dance is with the Royal Porcupine, in a pair of ugly black washerwoman boots that prove distinctly painful after only couple of waltzes (257).

Ultimately, then, the two paradigms—one of escape (The Lady of Shalott) and the other of tragic entrapment (Victoria of *The Red Shoes*)—don't quite fit. Joan, simply put, is not single-minded enough, either about disappearing from or about committing herself to her art. Both themes come together in chapter 34, as Joan realizes that she is not an "artist" as she had imagined all along. Instead, she is an "escape artist" (335). Just after realizing this, however, she tries one last time to resume the role of the artist figure, this time dancing alone. But as she raises her toes to dance, even as she remembers the dance from her childhood that makes her sure that "wings grew from [her] shoulders" (335), she finds herself dancing through the glass window. Not dead, like Victoria, in that grand suicidal gesture of the film's conclusion; Joan has merely gashed her feet. But, as she puts it at the end of the chapter: "How could I escape now, on my cut feet?" (336). The answer, of course, is that she can't. But, as the next three chapters reveal, she continues to try.

A GENRE-BASED READING

A "formalist" or genre-based reading is one that focuses on the form rather than content of a literary work—how it is written rather than what it is about. A formalist reading does not pay attention to the biographical context of the work. Rather, it pays close attention to the stylistic or "formal" devices that make up a specific genre, or kind, of narrative. Different genres can include the ghost story, the gothic novel, and the romance novel, for example. *Lady Oracle* at once embodies each of these genres at the same time as it parodies them.

Lady Oracle is a parody of a number of different kinds of narratives. It parodies, for example, narratives that describe an individual's search for an identity. Rather than *finding* an identity, that is, Joan sets out to *create* an identity, and she "fosters" more than one. Joan's mother seems to want Joan to make something of herself. Ironically, of course, she does just that.

It also parodies the narrative confession, where the narrator justifies her actions with the aim of receiving pardon from her confessor. Following the original model of the sinner's confession to a priest, the penitent usually expresses genuine remorse for misdeeds and makes a commitment to change his or her ways in the future. However, while Joan does make a confession to the reader about the labyrinthine deceptions she has masterminded, it is unclear whether she is genuinely remorseful and whether she will behave any differently in the future. The novel ends with Joan telling her story to the intruder, a journalist who has finally caught up with her in Italy, so that he will have something to show for his troubles. But the story she tells him (and surely readers must wonder about the story she tells them) also contains lies, though "not many" (344). Consequently, when the novel closes, Joan is still in the business of fabricating stories, and she is still in Italy honing the art of escape.

Most significantly, *Lady Oracle* parodies the gothic genre and has been described by Atwood herself as an " antigothic." That the novel challenges the gothic in particular is signaled by Joan's explanation of the "costume gothics" she writes. These, she explains in chapter 4, are a hybrid of two forms of novel: the gothic and the popular romance.

What is a gothic novel? Classics of this genre include Ann Radcliffe's *The Mysteries of Udolpho* (1794), Horace Walpole's *The Castle of Otranto* (1764), and Mathew Lewis's *The Monk* (1797). Characteristics of the traditional gothic include the aim of evoking terror through the use of mystery and, perhaps, the evocation of cruelty or horror; an eerie setting replete with gloomy medieval castles (perhaps dungeons and subterranean passages); and elements of the supernatural (including ghosts and mysterious disappearances). More recent gothic works have abandoned the specifically medieval setting but still try for an atmosphere of gloom, incorporate events that are uncanny or melodramatically violent, and aim to evoke a sense of fear. Examples include Mary Shelley's *Frankenstein* (1817); Charles Dickens's *Great Expectations* (1860), especially Miss Havisham's home; the works of William Faulkner, especially *Sanctuary* (1931) and *Absalom! Absalom!* (1936); and Emily Brontë's *Wuthering Heights* (1847). A particularly interesting example of gothic is Jane Austen's *Northanger Abbey* (1818), which itself is a parody of the genre (Abrams 72).

When the gothic form is combined with the popular romance, a fourth characteristic emerges: the source of gothic terror (experienced not by the reader, as in the pure gothic, but by the heroine) lies in the ambiguity and duplicity of the central male character. The heroine is unsure, until the moment of final revelation, whether he is hero or villain. Indeed, the plot of the popular romance (by which, within the context of *Lady Oracle*, we mean the dime-store or Harlequin variety) focuses on the initial loss of the heroine's identity. At the beginning of the romance narrative, that is, the heroine is often removed from a place of social stability. Charlotte, from *Stalked by Love,* for example, travels to the Redmond household to take up her position of jeweler. Precisely because the narrative turns on issues of identity and the need for and difficulty of identifying characters' motivations accurately, clothing and costumes play a crucial role. After all, clothing is often the most important clue as to an individual's identity. It is also one of the best forms of disguise. Other characteristics of the popular romance include: a happy ending, an exotic location, a conflict between the hero and heroine, the resolution of that conflict, and a love scene. Moreover, the popular romance is constructed in such a way that the reader knows more than the heroine. A good description of the popular romance genre, its female readership, and the social and political underpinnings of the industry, is provided by Janice Radway in her book, *Reading the Romance.*

When Joan acknowledges her desire to combine the two elements of "love" and "terror" in the title of her costume gothic, she is being explicit about the way her costume gothics are a hybrid between the two traditions of gothic and romance. Joan's costume gothics include: *Lord of Chesney Chase* (157), *Storm over Castleford* (182), and *Escape from Love* (162–64). Of course, we read most about *Stalked by Love.* Terror in this novel is foreshadowed by the maze, the drains, Charlotte's shredded clothing, and Redmond himself. Nevertheless, the expected outcome—that Felicia will die and Charlotte will get her man—is made clear (333). As with other passages of Joan's costume gothics, however, this begins to blend with the various intrigues of Joan's own life (335) so that, in the next two endings Joan imagines for the novel, the two worlds become inextricably linked. Most obviously, the female identities merge with Joan's (341), with the Fat Lady and Aunt Lou appearing as characters in *Stalked by Love.* Further, Joan's own life starts to follow the script of a costume gothic at the moment when she is threatened by an intruder (a gothic villain?), who quickly becomes an ally (a "nice man") and a potential lover ("he doesn't have a very interesting nose, but I have to admit that there is something about a man in a bandage" [345]).

Lady Oracle's humor is one of the most enjoyable outcomes of Atwood's parody of the gothic and the popular romance genres. But there is a more serious outcome as well: Atwood, through Joan, illustrates the dangers of gothic thinking. While Joan cannot see the "lesson from all of this" by the end of the novel (345), surely her readers can: being a gothic heroine isn't all it's cracked up to be. After all, Joan finds the role of the gothic heroine a restrictive one and spends much of her energy finding ways to escape.

6

Cat's Eye
(1988)

It is no coincidence that Atwood's oeuvre—fiction and poetry—is full of images of water and mirrors. These reflective surfaces in Atwood's writing provide an image of the way her writing works, as a medium that can reflect, or reflect upon, the world before it. Indeed, a useful way of describing the central strategies used by Atwood in her novels to expose and challenge would be to say they are different ways of reflecting or mirroring society and its literary traditions. In the artist novels (*Lady Oracle, Cat's Eye,* and, to a lesser degree, *Surfacing* and *Bodily Harm*), where women are cast in the role of artist rather than artist's model, we hear artists and storytellers reflect upon their art. In the dystopian novels depicting, as the word *dystopia* or "bad place" suggests, a nightmarish vision of the world (*Bodily Harm, The Handmaid's Tale,* and *Oryx and Crake*), our society is refracted in Atwood's fictional mirror, so that the reflection is a distorted one, the flaws of our society exaggerated as they are transposed into a different setting. Finally, in the villainess novels (*The Robber Bride, Alias Grace,* and *The Blind Assassin*), where Atwood's fiction often seems to invert the usual triumph of good over evil and powerful over powerless (a characteristic that disqualifies *Cat's Eye* from this particular category, although it is the clear precursor for *The Robber Bride*), we hear the reflections of the villainess herself and recognize her to be a reflection of those around her.

This suggestion that mirrors provide an analogy for art is nothing new. Whereas Plato suggested that artists could turn "a mirror round and round, " recreating a world that "would be appearances only" (Plato 22), Aristotle argued that "mimesis," or the way art reflects life, is a creative act, rather than mere replication, as art allows individuals to "learn and infer" about the world and themselves (Aristotle 44). Many critics suggest that art not only reflects life, but also has an obligation to do so. For example, Stephen Henighan in his recent book about contemporary Canadian literature, *When Words Deny the World,* argues that Canadian literature needs more novels that celebrate the contemporary urban realities of our day. Although his statement is linked to the contemporary moment, the sentiment behind it is Aristotelian in its origin.

Peculiar to Atwood's use of the mirror in her work is the way she empowers the mirror, often giving it a voice. In *Lady Oracle,* for example, Joan sees her life in terms of a mirror, and her readers begin to see Joan herself as a kind of mirror as her identity shifts to reflect changing circumstances. In "Tricks with Mirrors," the mirror proves itself to be highly—perhaps unnervingly—intelligent. In Atwood's poem, the speaker warns, "Don't assume [the mirror] is passive," merely performing tricks, because "mirrors are crafty" (*You Are Happy* 26). The lesson for Atwood's readers is that we must pay close attention not only to what the artist says about her art but also to what the art itself can say and, perhaps more importantly, do. For Atwood, after all, art's role is not just to imitate and entertain, but rather to do these things for a particular purpose: to reveal, challenge, and thereby dismantle the flaws in our society. The flaws spotlighted by *Cat's Eye* have to do with the male-dominated artistic tradition, one in which women tend to be models rather than artists and in which the classic novels describing an artist's coming of age focus on the male artist.

PLOT DEVELOPMENT

A novel about the development of an artist, Elaine Risely, *Cat's Eye* focuses on the nature and function of perspective in art: on the *eye* of the artist and the nature of the particular person or *"I"* who narrates this novel. Accordingly, its opening section involves two short chapters. The first opens a metaphysical discussion about the nature of time itself. Perhaps it is a "dimension" rather than a "line" (3). Is time pliable, something we can bend or shape at will? The second chapter introduces the central figure's preoccupation, even now that she is middle-aged, with her childhood girlfriend, Cordelia. Where is Cordelia now? Is she an older woman in a hospital, or perhaps a bag lady?

What prompts Elaine to think about Cordelia is the occasion for her being in Toronto, where a "retrospective" show of her art will be held in a downtown art gallery. She is staying with her ex-husband, Jon. Her current husband, Ben, remains in Vancouver, where she now lives with her two girls.

The second section of the novel, chapters 3 through 7, follows Elaine's reminiscences about her childhood until she settled in Toronto at the age of eight when her father took up a position in the Zoology Department at the University of Toronto. Elaine and her brother, Stephen, spent the summer months with her parents in the bush, where she remembers them collecting insects like their father and playing war in imitation of the adults then involved in WWII on the other side of the Atlantic. These memories are clouded by feelings of loneliness when she arrives in Toronto. For her eighth birthday, she wishes for friends with whom to play. When she settles into her new (and rather disappointing) house, she feels lonely in the bedroom she has to herself.

The predominant mood of part 3, chapters 8 through 15, is fear. In these chapters, Elaine remembers the early school years in Toronto. In the opening chapter, the attempted robbery of Elaine's purse foreshadows the kinds of vulnerability she feels as a young schoolgirl in this part of the novel. Whereas the older Elaine has learned how to deal effectively with threats (she brings her foot down, hard, on the wrist of the thief as she reaches beneath the wall of the changing-room cubicle), the younger Elaine has yet to go through her apprenticeship with Cordelia.

It all begins when the prevailing school culture, which separates girls from boys, gradually draws Stephen away from Elaine. Instead of playing with Stephen, she takes up with Carol Campbell. But the relationship is not entirely comfortable. Through Carol's eyes, Elaine realizes, her family is not entirely normal, and therefore neither is she. Unlike Elaine's own active mother, Grace's mother has a bad heart and takes rests most afternoons. Unlike Elaine's own parents, Carol's sleep in separate twin beds.

Whereas Elaine takes insects in her stride, for example, she notices that Stephen can cause quite a reaction in Carol by even talking about eating slugs. When Elaine watches Carol play with her friend Grace Smeath, cutting images from the Eaton's catalog, she realizes that theirs is a world with intricate rules and expectations, and one to which she is an outsider. She understands much better the games Stephen plays with his own friends. One favorite game is marbles. The novel's title derives from a particular kind of marble that Elaine prizes. She keeps her favorite cat's eye marble in a special red purse.

Chapter 13 describes the arrival of Cordelia, and chapters 14 and 15 indicate the layers of darkness that descend upon Elaine after her arrival. Elaine leaves Toronto for the summer with her family, and when she returns, she finds Grace and Carol in the same place, but with a third girl. When Elaine meets her, the connection is strong and quick. Elaine becomes part of a "circle of two" (79). Cordelia's sisters, Perdita and Miranda, are beautiful and accomplished. Cordelia, by comparison, is the youngest and vaguely disappointing sister. Within the group of girls, however, she takes on a leading role. When they walk along the wooden bridge together, it is Cordelia who awes them with tales of deadly nightshade and tells them that the water in the stream is made of decomposed dead people as it comes from the cemetery. Elaine's classroom hours turn bleak during this period as well because of the frightening Miss Lumley.

The ever-increasing darkness is signaled by the title of part 4, "Deadly Nightshade," a reference to the story told by Cordelia and to the persistent memory of the worst period of Elaine's childhood. Again, the subject that dominates part 4—Elaine's intimidation—is signaled by an episode in Elaine's present. Here, clad in a blue jogging suit, she feels awkward as she meets the impossibly chic Charna of Sub-Versions (the art gallery hosting her retrospective) and is decidedly on edge when interviewed by the feminist journalist, Andrea.

This episode seems to call forth the various memories of Elaine's childhood discomfort, such as when the worldly Cordelia exposes her to the mysteries of female sexuality (leg waxing, brassieres, and sanitary napkins) and human sexuality; when the Smeaths take her to church and then think her pagan as she starts to eat before they say grace; and when the brother she knows abandons her for a girlfriend. Finally in chapter 20, Elaine touches upon the most painful memory of all: the time when, playing Mary, Queen of Scots, she was lowered into the hole Cordelia had dug in her back garden. Disturbingly, Elaine can remember neither the details of what happened in that hole nor the details of such watersheds as her ninth birthday. In the novel's early section, Stephen had taught Elaine to see in the dark, but this darkness is of a different kind, and she can't see through it.

The present-day episode, in which the middle-aged Elaine is directed to the food area she seeks by a kindly salesperson at Simpsons, opens and sets the tone for part 5 and indicates that Elaine will find some help.

Although the sources of help and insight do appear in part 5, Elaine will only be able to make use of them later in her life.

Elaine remembers how she used to peel the skin off her feet, bite around her fingernails, and chew the ends of her hair when she was under Cordelia's influence. Chapter 22 details the minutiae of Cordelia's maliciousness to young Elaine: her exclusion from meetings during which the girls talk about her, her seat on a separate windowsill from them as they watch the Santa Claus parade from her father's Zoology Building, and the taunts on the way home from school. What makes it worse is Elaine's understanding that these are her best friends. Pure and consistent hatred would have made it simpler. But, confusingly, sometimes there are moments of relief. Either Cordelia relents and picks on Carol, or Elaine is able to stay home with her mother. She does keep going to church with the Smeaths, but essentially abandons any faith in friendship or a benevolent God.

What she does start to notice, however, are examples of different kinds of people who start the process of restoring her faith in humanity. The first is Mr. Bannerji, one of her father's students, who comes to the Risley house for Christmas dinner. The second is the Jewish Finestein family next door. Elaine is hired to wheel young Brian Finestein around the block but ultimately resigns because she is unsure whether she can keep Brian safe from "her friends." She spends her earnings on candy for those same "friends." Both Mr. Bannerji and Mrs. Finestein will appear in Elaine's later paintings as kinds of talismans, along with the cat's eye marble. For the moment, however, only Elaine's faith in the power of the cat's eye marble is of any practical help to her. Elaine feigns sickness often and feels relief when the family returns to the bush that summer. However, she is no longer interested in playing with Stephen when he suggests games that she "can't win" (165).

Elaine's situation worsens in part 6, "Cat's Eye," and builds to the moment of crisis and a turning point in part 7. In part 6, Elaine considers her options, most of them involving escape. Elaine feels that her mother, who is preoccupied with a miscarriage, is unable to help her, so she refuses even to open up to her. While in the basement of Simpsons in the opening episode of part 6, the middle-aged Elaine wonders what she would have done in her mother's place. Even now, even for someone with such a close acquaintance with abuse, she finds no obvious answer.

Part 6 describes Elaine's return from her summer away to find a new and more helpful teacher, the Scottish Miss Stuart, and the same gang of girls. Elaine does think about suicide; particularly, she contemplates stepping in front of Princess Elizabeth's car as she drives through Toronto.

But Elaine ultimately finds less dramatic forms of solace and escape. At Valentine's Day, when she notices that she receives more cards from boys than from the other three girls, she discovers that boys are her "secret allies" (185). She also discovers that she can step out of time when, at the Zoology Building one day, she faints. After this, Elaine teaches herself how to faint, and she also begins to spend more time outside of her body: "My eyes are open but I'm not there. I'm off to the side" (196). (This is reminiscent of Charis's method of coping with sexual abuse in *The Robber Bride*, when she learns to "split" herself into "two.")

Elaine's ability to envision escape is transformed into an ability to seek and perceive help when Elaine places her faith, in part 7, "Our Lady of Perpetual Help," in the Virgin Mary. Significantly, she decides to put her faith in a female deity. Does Elaine suspect that a male deity may not understand the peculiar dilemma in which she finds herself, as a girl among so-called girlfriends? Here, almost at the center of the novel, the power dynamic between Elaine and Cordelia is about to shift. This begins when Elaine overhears Mrs. Smeath and Aunt Mildred discussing her, and she realizes that they have known about, and condoned, the abuse all along. After deciding not to pray to God, Elaine discovers a picture of the Virgin Mary on the street. She begins to pray to Mary and will eventually turn to her when, in chapter 35, Cordelia forces her to fetch her hat from the icy-cold waters of the ravine. Clearly chilled by the cold and the ice, Elaine sees a vision of the Virgin Mary, who guides her out of the water to safety. When Elaine returns to school after two days at home, during which time the other girls have been reprimanded, she has become invulnerable to their taunts. When they try to torment her, Elaine just walks away. She also makes a new friend, Jill.

Part 7 begins the slow process during which Elaine regains the time she has lost. Once again, the Virgin Mary is connected with this process of salvation, when Elaine remembers seeing the Virgin of Lost Things when on a trip with Ben in Mexico. Lost to Elaine are not only the details of her "bad time" (as her mother describes it later [225]), but also the meaning of the talismans that saw her through it, including the cat's eye in its red purse, which she now stores in a trunk. Carol Campbell moves away. Grace and Cordelia skip a grade. Elaine has a boyfriend. Time moves in to cover the wounds and the memories.

On Elaine's first day of high school, she accompanies Cordelia, who has been held back, so is now in the same grade as Elaine. The tables seem to have turned since the last time the girls walked together. The school is significantly named Burnham High School, perhaps a reference to the

"Birnan" woods surrounding Macbeth's castle, woods that appear to move as the armies approach to conquer him. Now Cordelia's sisters, Perdie and Mirrie have both grown up, and they make fun of Cordelia. Cordelia begins to shoplift, stealing comic books.

Elaine, by comparison, seems to be returning to a normal life and is unconcerned about the things that previously worried her: that her brother was growing distant from her and that her mother was not like the other mothers in their matching outfits. She begins to babysit for the Finesteins again and to listen closely to Stephen's discussions about physics and the nature of time and the universe.

"Half a Face," the title of part 8, is revealed to be the title of a portrait of Cordelia in part 9. The portrait shows Cordelia, with fright in her eyes, and behind her, another face covered with a white cloth (Elaine's own). The opening section describes two other paintings as well, both of Mrs. Smeath, which depict her as vulnerable rather than powerfully antagonistic. In one, Mrs. Smeath is nude and bug-like; in the other, she is nude except for a pair of bloomers, reminiscent of the awful teacher, Miss Lumley.

As expected, then, the four chapters in part 8 depict Elaine's increasing control over Cordelia (she actually frightens her, deliberately, as they walk through the cemetery) and her dealing with her memories of Mrs. Smeath (as Elaine and Cordelia begin a game that makes fun of the Smeath family). Elaine gradually assumes a leadership role at school. She has a "mean mouth" (263), uses Cordelia for "target practice" (264), and is popular with boys because she understands them. Cordelia, by contrast, starts to do poorly at school and eventually fails, taking to drink. She seeks Elaine out, wanting to talk about old times, when she had the upper hand. Elaine understandably dodges her, wanting to escape before the darker memories surface.

Whereas the previous chapters describe Elaine's apprenticeship under Cordelia, "Life Drawing," part 10, describes Elaine's apprenticeship as an artist. It is introduced by Elaine's contemplation of her painting *Falling Women*, an illustration of three women falling from a bridge and a depiction of how men "unintentionally" cause women to fall.

The falling women in this part of the novel are Cordelia and the two who fall for the thirty-something Mr. Hrbik, the nighttime life-drawing instructor at the Toronto College of Art: first Susie, and later Elaine herself. Elaine is accepted into Mr. Hrbik's class on the basis of her limited portfolio and Mr. Hrbik's decision to "see what we can make of you" (305). During the day, Elaine is a scholarship student in Art History and Archeology at the University of Toronto. As during her school days, she feels self-conscious about not being quite like the others. When she grows her hair and starts to wear black, it indicates her desire to fit in with the Life Drawing crowd, with whom she goes out after art classes. She becomes increasingly distant from the university students and even teases the girls to prove to herself that she's not like them. About this time, Elaine moves into her parents' cellar. Stephen has moved out to California, and she lives a life largely independent of her parents. But by the end of the summer, after Susie has broken up with Mr. Hrbik (now called Josef), Elaine moves in with him and spends the summer working as a waitress at Swiss Chalet. Cordelia reappears, looking "distinguished" (336) with eyeliner and high cheekbones. Cordelia now works at the Stratford, a Shakespearean festival held each summer in a small town in Ontario called Stratford (after the town of Stratford-upon-Avon in Britain). But when Elaine goes to see *The Tempest* with the free ticket Cordelia supplies, she can't recognize Cordelia beneath the disguises.

Elaine takes up with Jon, a fellow art student who will become her husband. Jon offers Elaine a kind of escape, a sense of fun and freedom. Josef, Elaine realizes, as she thinks about it now from a mother's perspective, was an unhealthy relationship for such a young woman. Indeed, part 11, also entitled "Falling Women," focuses on the unhealthiness of the young women's situation and the ways they all, with the exception of Elaine, become fallen women. In the opening sequence, Elaine thinks she notices Cordelia only to realize that the person she thinks is Cordelia is actually a homeless lady.

Susie's relationship with Josef also ends in tragedy, as she appears at Elaine's one night, ill after a botched abortion performed with a knitting needle. Elaine takes Susie to the hospital and, now able to see Josef's true colors, ends their own relationship. Elaine pursues courses in advertising art and illustration, continues her degree, and gains a healthy understanding of the evolution of nude illustrations. When her father retires from the university and her parents move up north, Elaine gets her own apartment, spends more time with Jon, and gets a job in illustration. She hears from Stephen, who becomes an expert in his field, and gets married and divorced. When he comes to Toronto to give a lecture, Elaine tries to reconcile the adult Stephen with the brother she remembers. Elaine settles down with Jon, whom she later marries, and becomes pregnant with her daughter Sarah. Her painting style changes to include domestic objects: a wringer washer ("wringer" being the title of an earlier part of the novel) and Mrs. Smeath.

After about two years of marriage, Elaine's relationship with Jon disintegrates. By this time, she has become involved with a group of feminists. Being part of a group of women makes Elaine feel both nervous and powerful, sisterhood being a difficult concept for her, given her childhood experiences. In chapter 62, Elaine has her first art show, together with other women from her group, in a defunct supermarket. Her work gains particular attention from someone who resembles Grace Smeath, who throws ink on one of the paintings of Mrs. Smeath. This commotion actually increases the show's impact and popularity.

Elaine also visits Cordelia at the Dorothy Lyndwick Rest Home where she is staying after an attempted suicide with drugs. Cordelia asks Elaine to help her escape. Angry at being asked, Elaine refuses, but is later disturbed by having not done something to help.

In part 12, "One Wing," the adult Elaine wanders by Josef's house, thinking about the film he made and about how women were never real to him. She meets Jon for drinks, and they go back to the apartment and have sex one last time. But the rest of part 12 returns to the time when her marriage was disintegrating, when Jon cheated on her, and when Elaine worked to meet the rent but never had time for her own painting. She, like Cordelia, fell into a depression and attempted suicide. After that, she took Sarah to Vancouver, where she started painting again and joined a group of women artists. This group was far more militant than the first one, made up of lesbians and radical feminists, with whom she didn't quite feel comfortable. It was in Vancouver that she met Ben, with whom she has a second daughter, Anne, and a stable and happy relationship.

If chapter 13 contains the moment when Elaine is lowered into the dark pit in Cordelia's back yard, part 13 takes Elaine back into the dark heart of her childhood memories. In part 13, "Picoseconds," Elaine returns to the neighborhood of her childhood. Stephen's death in a hostage situation on an airplane is now five years in the past. When she identifies the body, Elaine remembers how she realized that she would get older and that he would not. Her parents die as well, her father suddenly, and her mother of a slower progressing disease. When Elaine visits her mother, she raises the subject of the "bad time," but Elaine still can't remember the details. Only afterwards, when she goes through a trunk (symbolic, in Atwood's work, of the subconscious) with her mother and finds her plastic purse and her cat's eye marble, do the memories flood back. At that moment, she "sees [her] life entire" (449). Part 18 ends with Elaine looking for her old school only to find a new one in its place. The old order, in other words, has given way to the new.

Part 14, "Unified Field Theory," initiates the conclusion of the novel, as Elaine looks over the paintings in her retrospective. Her art is arranged chronologically, and Elaine examines her paintings and describes several of them. Although the event goes well, Elaine realizes that she is disappointed that Cordelia has not come. That Elaine is bothered by her absence makes her realize that Cordelia still has a hold on her and that she has not been able to put Cordelia entirely behind her.

In the last part, "The Bridge," Elaine goes to the ravine. She realizes, now, that she never actually saw the Virgin Mary. Rather, she saw a vision of the younger Cordelia. For Elaine, Cordelia was both her tormentor and her savior. On the plane back to Vancouver, Elaine watches two old women and concludes that this is what makes her sad—that she will never have this kind of companionship in her older years, the intimacy, even "giggling" (478) between two longtime friends. The novel closes with Elaine looking out into the moonless and star-filled night (the stars, of course, reflections of explosions that happened many years before), realizing that she has traveled in time since the first time she and Cordelia encountered one another.

NARRATIVE STRUCTURE

Cat's Eye is tightly controlled, almost symmetrical in its shape. In chapter 36, for example, Elaine discovers her freedom from Cordelia by walking away. It takes as many chapters for Elaine to realize, in chapter 72, that the adult Cordelia has walked away from her. These two characters are, after all, like opposite sides of the same coin. The first half of the novel traces Cordelia's growing control over the young Elaine, whereas the second half of the novel traces Elaine's rise to power in their relationship and Cordelia's collapse.

This shifting power dynamic between these two central characters is framed within two larger narratives: one, in the novel's present, in which the adult Elaine returns to the city of her childhood for a retrospective exhibition of her art; the other, Elaine's and Stephen's ongoing metaphysical discussion about the nature of time and space, and therefore of memory. Each major section in the novel is framed by a reference to this second larger discussion of time. The novel opens, for example, with Elaine describing Stephen's (and before him, Stephen Hawking's) notion that time may not be as simple a concept as we all think. This introduction—which states that time is a dimension rather than a simple line that moves from past to present, something one can look through "like a series of liquid transparencies" (3)—guides the way we come to understand Elaine's past as having influenced her present.

However, if the narrative of time illustrates the way Elaine's past impinges on her present, the narrative of Elaine's present-day experience in Toronto (episodes that introduce each part of the novel and set the tone for the chapters to follow) illustrates the way Elaine's present can influence her thinking about her past.

The novel's sections are given the titles of Elaine's paintings. Consequently the "biographical" context for a painting appears in the relevant section of Atwood's novel, and the painting itself is described in part 14, in which Elaine describes the paintings that hang on the walls of the gallery. In this way, particular objects take on great resonance. Of these, the cat's eye takes on particular significance. The title of a painting (Elaine's self-portrait), the title of a section and of the novel itself, and the name of Elaine's prized marble that becomes a kind of talisman for her, "cat's eye" becomes an anagogic metaphor—an object that stands for a number of related things.

CHARACTER DEVELOPMENT

Elaine and Cordelia, the two central characters of *Cat's Eye*, have much in common: a childhood in the same Toronto suburb, a gift for storytelling, an adult life clouded by an attempted suicide, and ambivalent memories of one another. Elaine is the novel's central protagonist and narrator, while Cordelia is the novel's antagonist. That Elaine is so obviously the victim of Cordelia in her early years, and that she genuinely regrets her unwillingness to help Cordelia later on, disguises the fact that *Cat's Eye* contains many of the elements of Atwood's villainess novels: most significantly, a narrator who is acutely aware of the power dynamics in her interpersonal relationships and able to learn how to gain the upper hand. However, such initiation can also be compared with the coming-of-age narrative, often described as bildungsroman, and more specifically in Elaine's case, with the *künstlerroman*, or the narrative of an artist's development.

Elaine's development as an individual includes a number of pivotal moments in her apprenticeship as a girl: her exposure to the culture of small girls in the 1940s (chapter 10); her exposure to the nuances of difference in race and behavior within Canada's middle class (chapter 14); and her gradual awareness of sexuality, first through contemplation of Mrs. Lumley's "bloomers" (chapter 15), then through conversations with the other girls (chapter 17). Pivotal moments in her apprenticeship under

Cordelia trace the way Elaine becomes familiar with notions of codified behavior and punishment for deviance, as when she is lowered into the hole in Cordelia's backyard (chapter 20), when she discovers the many things women should *not* do as she flips through women's magazines (chapter 26), and when she learns the Christian gospel of retribution at church with the Smeaths (chapter 34). The turning point comes when, abandoned in the ravine, Elaine imagines the Virgin Mary telling her to "[g]o home" (213). From this point on, Elaine is able to ignore Cordelia and to begin her growth as an independent and resourceful individual.

Pivotal to Elaine's subsequent growth is her development as an artist. We trace her entrance into the Life Drawing class at the Toronto College of Art, her first art exhibition with a group of women in Toronto, her later membership in a more feminist group of artists in Vancouver, and her eventual retrospective exhibition in the Toronto gallery Sub-Versions. Her detailed memory hampered by gaps, Elaine's art draws on the resonance of particular objects, which she paints in great detail. That is, Elaine begins to paint things that aren't there; she draws on memories that she can't place (chapter 60), even before she looks into the newly discovered cat's eye marble and sees her "life entire" (in chapter 69).

If Elaine escapes Cordelia's influence after her ordeal in the ravine, the balance of power does not actually shift until Elaine, when walking in the cemetery with Cordelia, terrifies her with a story of vampires (261–62). When she realizes that Cordelia is truly frightened, Elaine also realizes that she has become the "stronger" of the two. After this, Elaine witnesses Cordelia's journey toward vulnerability: she is expelled from St. Sebastian's school, fails a grade, and takes up shoplifting (chapters 38 and 39); fails a zoology exam and doesn't care, indeed lacks interest in school generally (chapter 44); confesses to Elaine her sense of vulnerability at home that first prompted her to dig holes in her backyard and also to induce herself to vomit (chapter 45); takes up smoking and drinking (chapter 46); and is finally institutionalized after a suicide attempt (chapter 63).

Despite their different trajectories, however, Cordelia and Elaine function as twins in this novel. As in the comic-book stories, in which everything contains its mirror opposite (237–38), Cordelia and Elaine complement one another. Elaine is present, in the form of a face covered by a white cloth, in her portrait of Cordelia (255). Perhaps Elaine's sense that she is a vampire provides another way of thinking about their relationship (261–62): each one draws strength from the other. We never see a time, in this novel, where both are strong and independent of one another.

Toward the end of the novel, Elaine comes to understand the reciprocity of her relationship with her tormentors. There are moments when Elaine's eyes meet those of her tormentors, and in those moments she achieves a kind of recognition in the similarity of their positions. For example, Elaine achieves a measure of forgiveness when she sees her own eyes in her portrait of Mrs. Smeath (457). Similarly, when she discovers an image of Cordelia in the ravine at the very end of the novel, Elaine realizes that the fear felt by her younger self mirrored the fear of Cordelia herself.

Other characters play particular roles in Elaine's development, roles that are clarified in her paintings: the bad mother (Mrs. Smeath), the good mother (her own), and an ambivalent group of peers (Carol, Grace, and Cordelia). As well, Elaine sees three individuals as playing inspirational roles in her formation as an artist. These three appear in her painting *The Three Muses*: Mrs. Finestein, Miss Stuart (the kind Scottish teacher), and Mr. Bannerji.

In this novel about the need for women to gain a voice and identity independent of their male counterparts, men play a particularly negative role. In the world of heterosexual middle-class life of the 1940s and 1950s, men are absent during the day and present when it is dark. Their role is dark as well. Cordelia's father rules over the women of his household, and Carol's father uses his belt buckle when he scolds her. Elaine's own experience with men suggests that subsequent generations have not improved the model. Josef impregnates Susie and refuses to take much responsibility, and Jon is a philanderer. Although Ben seems to be a good man, we hear very little about him. Generally, men play either an antagonistic or a passive role in this novel. As such, they are contemporary examples of a group of individuals who have either systematically reduced women to silence or, through their own silence, condoned it.

THEMES AND ALLUSIONS

The novel makes a number of references to Shakespeare, all related to Cordelia. She is the props manager for a production of *Macbeth* (where her replacement of a rotten cabbage for a good one transforms the tragic tone to one of inappropriate humor) and later appears in a production of *Macbeth* at Stratford. Her sisters, Perdita and Miranda, are named for Shakespearean protagonists. Cordelia's own name reminds us of the faithful daughter of King Lear, who chooses to say nothing when her father asks for verbal evidence of his daughter's love. Instead, she supports him when he is in dire need. But this genuine proof of her love comes too late for any reward for her. The "nothing" that Cordelia says in response to

King Lear's question haunts the characterization of Atwood's Cordelia. Cordelia makes Elaine feel like nothing, because this is the way she feels in her own household. Cordelia eventually does become nothing, as she disappears entirely from Elaine's life. Elaine's disappearances as she faints or steps sideways in time, by contrast, are only temporary. Interestingly, in earlier drafts of *Cat's Eye*, Atwood has Cordelia appear before Elaine at the end of the novel.

The reference to the severed head in *Macbeth* is also an example of the many heads in this novel. The first one appears in the novel's epigraph, taken from Eduardo Galeano's *Memory of Fire: Genesis*, and describes not only a beheading but also, more significantly, the way the soul of the beheaded enters the body of its murderer. Elaine dreams of a severed head at the end of chapter 44, imagining it wrapped in a white tea towel (like the one appearing in her painting *Half a Face*). In this dream, Elaine seems to have an early understanding of the way Cordelia will always be a part of her.

Another allusion (or reference to a well-known character or object of art) in the novel is to Van Eyck's famous painting *The Arnolfini Marriage*. Elaine, as an artist, becomes fascinated with the way it provides an example of an artist's successful rendering of a reflective surface (366). The painting itself provides an image of a betrothed couple and, in the background, a pier glass—or convex mirror—that reveals two other individuals. A line beside the mirror reads: "Johannes de Eyck fuit hic. 1434." Consequently, viewers have identified the man in the pier glass as the artist himself. This painting provides a metaphor for Elaine's own portraits (which contain depictions of the individual's face, as well as objects signifying pivotal influences on them), and for Atwood's novel itself.

A THEMATIC READING

New Criticism changed the way literature was discussed in universities during the 1960s and 1970s. It focused on the text itself—scrutinizing the details of the text's themes and images—rather than on its context—the author's biography, for example, or its reception by different critics and audiences. A thematic reading of the kind that follows here, involving close scrutiny or explanation of an individual text's themes, is what Russell Brown calls "explicative thematics" (644)—as opposed to "comparative thematics," which compare the themes of different texts in a particular canon. As such, explicative thematics is a form of New Criticism, since it focuses exclusively on the text itself and on the way in which different instances of the theme serve to amplify and direct a particular reading.

The central image of Atwood's *Cat's Eye* is clearly the cat's eye marble— a blue cat's eye marble—which reappears a number of times during the course of Elaine's turbulent journey toward maturity. When it is introduced in chapter 12 (66), where Elaine elaborates on the game of marbles itself, its value seems to be its beauty. Although she does play marbles at school, risking the loss of her cat's eye marbles, she never actually risks losing the blue one. Instead, she keeps it in her red plastic purse. (Her brother, a far better shot, hides his own marbles in a glass jar that he buries deep in the ravine.) However, the cat's eye seems to serve another function as well since when Elaine is without it, she seems peculiarly vulnerable. When she goes to church, where she first exposes herself to the pious judgments of the Smeaths, she leaves it behind and takes a nickel for the collection box instead (101). This heralds the beginning of that dark winter, one in which she is lowered into the hole in Cordelia's backyard (113). When spring comes, bringing "marble season" with it, Elaine retrieves her special cat's eye. She describes the blue in it like "something frozen in ice" (151),which seems to anticipate the ordeal she will soon have to face, as she tries to retrieve her hat from beneath the icy waters of the ravine. By spring, Elaine understands that the cat's eye marble has become powerful and that it can empower her. Sometimes, she says, she "can see the way it sees" (151). Its power, of course, is that it models a way for Elaine to see her situation differently. As something that can't hear, it embodies something upon which the girls' words of torment have no effect.

During the summer, the power of the cat's eye becomes something that Elaine can internalize. In a dream, she sees it fall from the sky and imagines that it "passes" right into her (155). By the time she goes back to school, she sees the marble as a talisman and keeps it carefully in her pocket from where it can look "out through bone and cloth with its impartial gaze" (166). Imagining the impartiality of the marble, Elaine is able to neutralize her obvious sensitivity to the three girls, her terror of their strength. Now she is able to see them as mere "puppets" (166). At this stage of the novel, then, the cat's eye marble represents a particular way of seeing: from a distance, with a cold impartiality.

In the next half of the novel, however, it comes to represent not only a way of seeing, but also what Elaine saw during those traumatic years of her childhood. When the turning point comes, as Cordelia throws her blue hat down into the ravine (200), enacting the very scene anticipated when Elaine stared into the blue at the center of her cat's eye marble (151), there is significantly no mention of the marble itself. Elaine's ability to see, indeed to remember what she has seen, vanishes in the ravine. Only many years later, as she and her mother are tidying the house, does Elaine discover her red purse and the marble inside it. Her mother thinks it is one of Stephen's, and Elaine does not correct her. What she does do is look into it—not through it, or as if she were seeing from its perspective. At that moment, she regains all the memories she had lost, she sees "her life entire" (420).

That is, the marble itself vanishes for all the years between Elaine's illness after the incident in the ravine, and her mother's illness toward the end of her life. It resurfaces in the two last paintings in Elaine's five-painting retrospective. The fourth painting is actually entitled *Cat's Eye*, and, as the artist's self-portrait, it attests to Elaine's recognition of the way she was formed by her close association with that special marble—the way she imagined it seeing things and what it saw (430). There is no marble in the painting. Instead, there is a pier glass that, like the one in Van Eyck's painting, reveals something that is not in the painting itself: the three little girls. Elaine's painting, then, suggests that those three girls are as absent (as characters from Elaine's past) as they are present (integral to who she has become).

The cat's eye marble does appear in the last painting, *Unified Field Theory* (430), which depicts the Virgin of Lost Things holding the marble in front of her, in the place where the cold little girl had once seen a red heart (200). Beneath her is the "night sky," but Elaine explains that the darkness hides all the things that are there as well: things in the "underside of the ground" (431). This last painting is, in other words, a depiction of darkness. What the Virgin and the marble she holds represent is Elaine's recovery of her memory of the dark time of her childhood and also of the value of seeing that darkness.

7

The Handmaid's Tale
(1985)

The Handmaid's Tale provides an example of the second way in which Atwood exposes the double standards associated with gender in our society. In *Cat's Eye,* as in the other artist novels (*Surfacing, Lady Oracle*), Atwood casts a woman in the role of artist rather than of muse or model, traditional figures of inspiration for art, and traces her development of a particularly woman-centered aesthetic. In *The Handmaid's Tale,* as in the other dystopian novels (ones that paint a picture of a nightmarish world, either imagined [as in *Oryx and Crake*] or largely real [as in *Bodily Harm*]), Atwood changes the setting so as to exaggerate and expose some of the failings of our society, including disregard for the environment and the inequitable distribution of power between individuals. Each of these three dystopian texts, however, is very different, which makes it all the more difficult to choose a representative text for analysis. *Oryx and Crake* is an anomaly in Atwood's oeuvre, both because it is the only novel narrated entirely by a male character and because feminist issues are not of primary concern. *Bodily Harm* is another anomaly, as the only novel in Atwood's oeuvre that places its emphasis squarely on Canadian international relations and postcolonial concerns, in a narrative that exposes the inequities of both race and gender. *The Handmaid's Tale,* which takes aim at gender inequality, is, consequently, more representative of Atwood's work as a whole.

Three other reasons justify its selection for close analysis. First, it is perhaps Atwood's best-known novel of her midcareer. Next, although its feminist and ecological themes are consistent with the rest of her oeuvre, its speculative and futuristic style marks a dramatic turning point in Atwood's fiction, one that introduces a new willingness to move beyond the realistic Canadian locales that dominated her early work. Finally, although Atwood had incorporated satire in her earlier work (*The Edible Woman, Murder in the Dark,* and *Power Politics*), *The Handmaid's Tale* is Atwood's first full-length satire. What makes it particularly interesting, though, is the fact that it is a satire written by a woman, since "satire," as Lorraine York quite rightly puts it, "is gendered male" (43). Further, although *The Handmaid's Tale* can be seen as a response to George Orwell's novel *1984*, (uncharacteristically for Atwood) it does seem to abide by the conventions of the genre in which it is written.

PLOT DEVELOPMENT

The novel is composed of 15 sections, with 1 additional section entitled "Historical Notes." Sections, with only one exception, alternate between descriptions of night and daytime. Consequently, odd-numbered sections (parts 1, 3, 7, 9, 11, 13, and 15) bear the same title: "Night." The one exception is part 5, entitled "Nap," which separates sections describing one long and particularly traumatic day.

In the first section, only one chapter long, the female narrator and a group of other women are contained in what used to be a school gymnasium. This gymnasium is policed by older women or "Aunts" with cattle prods and guards or "Angels" with guns. Some readers may recognize that, as the names of the various Aunts are provided, they have the names of famous figures of North American consumer society: Aunt Helena (Helena Rubenstein), Aunt Lydia (Lydia Pinkerton), Aunt Elizabeth (Elizabeth Arden), Aunt Betty (Betty Crocker), and Aunt Sarah (Sarah Lee). Silently, while in their beds, facing one another so as to lip-read, the prisoners exchange their names: Alma, Janine, Dolores, Moira, and June. Constance Rooke, in a convincing feat of detective criticism, argues that the narrator's name is June although, like Atwood's Surfacer, she never reveals her name to the reader. We know her only by the name she has been given, "Offred," because she belongs to the Commander "Fred" (Rooke 176)

In part 2, "Shopping," chapter 2 is narrated by the same individual, who describes her own red dress (clearly a kind of uniform) and, as she catches sight of it in the pier glass hanging beside the stairs, her face framed in the white wings of her headdress. She mentions details of "the Commander's" household, including the way time is structured by bells and the way she is not part of the inner circle of the household that consists of Cora, the cook, and Rita, the housekeeper or "Martha," with her green uniform. The narrator thinks of Luke, her husband from "before."

Chapter 3 provides a description and meditation about the Commander's wife, a blond woman wearing "the Wife's" blue uniform, whom the narrator recognizes as Serena Joy, a television star from the Sunday morning religious programming of the "time before." She bears a striking resemblance to Tammy Faye Baker, wife of the televangelist Jim Baker in the 1980s.

Chapter 4 introduces a series of moments when Offred engages with those around her. First, Nick, "a Guardian" and the family's chauffeur, winks at her after he catches Offred looking at him. Then Offred starts a cautious conversation with her shopping partner, "Ofglen." Finally, she exchanges a brief clandestine glance with one of the Guardians who checks her shopping pass. She notices him blush and feels the gaze of the Guardians as she walks away, consciously moving her hips, relishing the power of making them watch. The Guardians work in pairs, in part to prevent such encounters from going any further. There are no longer films or magazines, no outlets for sexual activity.

The society is gradually identified as the Republic of Gilead, and whatever revolution took place to establish it seems to be ongoing. Offred, as a Handmaiden whose duty is to provide the Commander with a child, is the most protected member of this society. However, she is not pregnant, and in her discussion with the Commander's wife, we learn that this is her third placement. While shopping, she encounters the pregnant Ofwarren, who turns out to be Janine from "The Red Centre." She also encounters a group of Japanese tourists arriving to take photographs in Westernized clothing of the kind Offred herself used to wear. Through a translator, they ask if Offred and Ofglen are happy. Offred replies in the affirmative thinking, "What else can I say?"

That they are not happy becomes very clear when, in chapter 6, they encounter a nightmarish scene: the Wall, upon which are displayed those hanged for "war" crimes, mostly abortionists, punished retroactively for acts that were, in the time before, legal. Their faces are covered with white cloth. Offred feels a slight "tremor" in her partner, but the two say nothing to one another.

Part 3, the second of seven sections entitled "Night," contains Offred's

in the Red Centre, when Moira revealed her plan to forego vitamins so as to get scurvy and escape. Serena Joy begins to cry and then, incongruously, farts. If this Ceremony can regulate bodily function, it cannot eliminate it.

Sexual intercourse doesn't take place until chapter 16, with the narrator held between the legs of Serena Joy on her four-poster bed. Everyone is, essentially, fully clothed. Intercourse itself takes place without kissing, which is forbidden, and without any sense of pleasure or possibility of pleasurable orgasm for either party. Offred is summarily dismissed by Serena Joy the moment the Ceremony ends rather than after the requisite ten minutes of rest, and Offred wonders which of the two women hate this more.

Joys, in the Republic of Gilead, are clandestine, like the secrecy of stolen butter that Offred uses as a moisturizer on her face, like the object she wants to steal from the household. Whom she encounters, as she fingers the dried daffodil she eventually decides to take, is Nick. Breathless, they embrace with a longing born of withheld desire. But the encounter is brief. They pull apart, shaking with sexual tension, and Nick relays his message that the Commander wants to see her, "tomorrow" (93).

In the next "Night" section, part 7, Offred thinks about the man in her past life: Luke. She imagines three endings to the story of their escape: that Luke was shot dead and is still in the bush; that he was not killed, but is now imprisoned; that he escaped with their daughter, reached some underground organization, and will send word to her one day. Offred believes that one of these must be the real ending, and further, that she can deal with whichever one proves to be true.

Rather than imagining the past, Offred, in part 8, turns her attention to the details of the present. This chapter describes a birth ceremony, introducing its theme with Offred's morning meal of boiled eggs (symbols of birth) and toast. The "Birthmobile" collects her after breakfast and takes her to the house of Janine, now Ofwarren. The chances of a successful birth, Offred knows, are slim. Pollution in the time "before" has rendered most people sterile. Even Offred's own mother, who had Offred when she was 37, knew there were risks. At one point, Offred remembers one of the movies they watched at the Red Centre, one in which she recognized her young mother, herself a zealous feminist (113). Behind her is the slogan "Take Back the Night" as well as others: "Freedom to Choose. Every Baby a Wanted Baby. Recapture Our Bodies" (113).

In the house where Janine lives, all the Wives and all the Handmaids perform the birthing ceremony. The narrator recognizes her shopping partner, Ofglen, among the crowd of women. Both Janine and the Wife are treated as though they are in labor. In the commotion of the rhythmic chants of "pant," then "push," and the spiked grape juice, the Handmaids have a chance to talk to one another. She asks someone, who says her name is Alma, if she has seen Moira. As Janine's labor intensifies, she and the Wife are moved to the double birthing chair, and the Wife is given the honor of naming and holding the baby after she is born. After the birth scene, Offred thinks of the women's society her mother had wanted. How close and how far is the Republic of Gilead from what she had imagined?

Offred learns something else from Alma (via Dolores, via Janine, via Aunt Lydia): the story of what happened to Moira. One day, Moira managed to dismantle the toilet at the Red Centre, take Aunt Elizabeth hostage, exchange clothes with her, and eventually escape. Such daring makes Moira the "fantasy" of the other Handmaids, the proof that freedom can be attained. For Aunt Lydia, who tells Janine the story in order to gain information about Moira's whereabouts, it is a problem in the system that must be rectified.

Exhausted after the "Birth Day," Offred almost forgets her arranged rendezvous with the Commander that evening. Curiously, rather than the sexual request she (and Atwood's reader) anticipates, when she enters the Commander's office, which is full of the books now forbidden in Gilead, Offred is invited to play Scrabble. The contraband in Gilead is not sex but words. She wins the first game and then, just to be safe, gives the Commander the second game. When, at the end of the evening, he asks for a kiss, another element forbidden in their formal relationship at the Ceremony, she consents. However, Offred's telling of the story seems to contain some equivocation. Having described how she, like Moira, thought about dismantling the toilet at the Commander's house, she later admits that she thought no such thing. Similarly, she acknowledges discrepancies in her account of her encounter with the Commander. Clearly, Offred is, after all, in control of this story.

At the time of the next "Night" section (part 9), Offred is well aware that her situation has changed. But is it really for the better? She remembers a television interview with a mistress of one of the supervisors of the Nazi concentration camps during WWII. Although she never mentioned that she loved this man, she did speak of him as human rather than monstrous. Offred also recalls that this woman committed suicide the week after that interview.

Offred's reaction to the horrible ludicrousness of her situation is itself bizarre. When alone in her room, she erupts into almost uncontrollable laughter—hysteria—and tries to silence it by hiding in the closet. When Cora brings her breakfast the following morning, though, she is terrified to find the bed not slept in. Screaming, she drops the breakfast tray, anticipating a suicide like that of Offred's predecessor.

But Offred does not seem inclined toward suicide. Her resilience is evident in part 10, "Soul Scrolls." She begins to visit the Commander more frequently, two or three nights a week. They play Scrabble, and he begins to bring her things, which she can touch and use while in his office: a *Vogue* magazine and hand lotion. He never asks for more than the one kiss and the game of Scrabble. He plays so well that Offred now realizes he had let her win that first game. When he explains that he does not do these things with his wife because they now share little in common, Offred is struck by how familiar that sounds. Is she thinking of what Luke, who had been married at the time he first met Offred, had told her?

At the next Ceremony, Offred thinks about how her relationship to the Commander has changed due to their meetings over the past three weeks. She is shy with the Commander, and her hatred of Serena Joy is now mixed with jealousy and guilt. The Commander almost gives it away by raising his hand, as if to touch her. Offred moves his hand away quickly and rebukes him at their next meeting. He apologizes, explaining that he finds it "impersonal" (152). There is a naïveté about the Commander, despite his obviously high rank in this new society.

By contrast, Ofglen proves herself to be acutely aware of the way the Republic of Gilead works. As she and Offred walk by "Soul Scrolls," their eyes meet, in the glass of the prayer-printing establishment. That unflinching exchange of glances prompts their mutual confession as nonbelievers and Ofglen's subsequent acknowledgment of an underground group of dissidents. Their conversation is interrupted when a large black van with a painted eye, the symbol of the "Eyes" or investigation unit, pulls up nearby to arrest a man by force, in a scene very reminiscent of George Orwell's *1984*.

Chapter 28 describes the way the Revolution progressed. First, paper money was eliminated so that bank and identification records were all computerized. Next, companies were told to dismiss their female employees. Finally, women were not allowed to access their own bank accounts (so Offred couldn't even pay for her packet of cigarettes). Offred's immediate reaction was to phone her mother and then Moira. Moira, who by then was openly lesbian, decided to go underground. Offred stayed at home, housekeeping, and opted to follow Luke's advice about not protesting. Her mother would have certainly chosen to do something different. Hauntingly, it strikes Offred that Luke was not entirely unhappy with having her at home, dependent upon him.

Offred becomes suspicious of the motives of the men in her present life as well. She watches Nick in chapter 28, clearly intrigued with him and with his willingness to "pimp" himself for the Commander. More troubling, when she asks the Commander about the phrase inscribed in her cupboard, he explains that it was a Latin joke that he and his schoolboy friends had created, meaning "Don't let the bastards grind you down." Recognizing the Commander as the original source for her predecessor's phrase of defiance, she realizes that she is not the first Handmaid with whom he has done this. Offred confronts the Commander, who tells her that the previous tenant of her room also visited him. In the end, Offred's predecessor committed suicide by hanging herself in the closet. This information explains Cora's scream on the morning she found Offred in the closet. It also further exposes the bleakness of her situation. When "Night" returns, in part 11, Offred thinks of death (of Luke killing their cat on the night they tried to escape), and of the futility that underlies so many of our actions, so much of life (given their capture). Eventually in despair, a nonbeliever, Offred turns to prayer.

Part 12, "Jezebel's" (details of the Biblical character of this name can be found in 1 Kings 16–21), describes Offred's increasingly complicated transactions with those around her. Chapter 31 begins with Ofglen's disclosure of her group's password—Mayday—a word she had used during their earliest discussion to probe Offred's level of knowledge. Next, Serena Joy proposes that Offred sleep with Nick since, because she is not yet pregnant by the Commander, her life will be in danger and Serena Joy will be without a child. Offred agrees. In return, Serena Joy suggests that she might be able to get Offred a picture of her little girl. Offred wonders how Serena Joy knows about her daughter. Finally, in chapter 32, we see a small but significant transaction: Offred obtains a single match from Rita and, in return, she gives her a compliment. That match is the only weapon Offred has in her possession during the entire novel, although it is never used.

Offred's interactions with the Commander also become more complicated. He starts drinking in her presence, holding her hand, cheating at Scrabble. She watches, asks questions of him, and comes to understand that the Republic of Gilead was a solution to a problem experienced by men in the time before: the lack of things to "work for" or "fight for," an inability to feel (198).

Offred and Ofglen go to a Prayvaganza. Women's Prayvaganzas are for marriages, and this one involves 20 new brides (none more than 14 years old) marrying 20 Angels. Offred thinks about love, the way it has disappeared from Gilead's concept of marriage. Kneeling at the back of the Prayvaganzas, Ofglen and Offred take the opportunity to talk about Janine, who enters with a new Handmaid partner. Ofglen tells Offred that the baby has died since the Birth Day, that it was Janine's second difficult birthing (the first being an eight-month miscarriage), and that Janine felt the failure was hers since the father was a doctor. Offred remembers the nervous breakdown Janine had at the Red Centre and remembers Moira bringing her back to reality by slapping her. Ofglen also mentions her knowledge of Offred's meetings with the Commander and asks that she obtain information for her group. How does Ofglen know about their relationship, the reader wonders? Could Nick belong to their group?

The memories of Luke and their escape keep coming back. Offred cries in her room, remembering their attempted escape, the "foolproof" passport identifying their marriage as legal (second marriages were no longer legal in Gilead), the moment when Luke came back (too quickly) to the car as the border guard reached for his phone. Interrupting Offred's painful recollections, Serena Joy knocks and enters with a picture of her daughter, now older and dressed in what looks like a confirmation dress. The photo must be returned, but it is evidence that she is still alive.

At their next secret encounter, the Commander gets Offred to put on a sequin and feather costume dress, as well as makeup (all black-market items). Nick drives them to an officer's club called Jezebel's. The Commander's instructions suggest that this is not the first time he has done this. The club is full of women, prostitutes from the time before, as well as executives who prefer this life to the others available. She accepts his offer of a drink and has a gin and tonic. Waiting for the Commander to return, Offred looks around the room and is astonished to see Moira. Barely recognizable in her own costume, Moira also notices Offred and, using their "old signal," silently arranges a meeting in the bathroom (225).

Chapter 38 describes their conversation in the washroom, as Moira tells the story of her escape. Thanks to the help of the Quakers, Moira is smuggled from family to family, traveling the "Underground Femaleroad" (a name that echoes that of the Underground Railroad that took slaves from the Southern United States northward toward Canada). Eventually the "Eyes" caught them (Moira and the Quaker couple who were then helping her, presumably those Offred had seen on the television news broadcast in the Commander's house) near the border. The "Eyes" took Moira for themselves for a time, then showed her a film about the Colonies, a version of concentration camps, then offered her a choice between Jezebel's and the Colonies. Jezebel's, Moira explains, is full of women "who don't think much of men" (234). What eventually becomes of her, however, Offred never knows. It is the last time she sees her.

The Commander and Offred go to a room at the club. It's like a hotel room from "before." The bathroom has small soaps, individually wrapped. They sleep together, he hoping that she might actually enjoy it. But she is inert, unable to be any different with him in private than she has been in the highly public Ceremony.

By midnight, she is back at the house, and Serena Joy comes to get her for the planned rendezvous with Nick. Serena Joy waits in the kitchen. Offred describes her meeting with Nick twice: in one version it is romantic, in the other version merely friendly, acknowledging that she will never reconstruct it fully. But it is clear that they have sexual intercourse and that she enjoys it. Both of these facts make her feel that she has betrayed Luke.

Her betrayal extends to those around her in part 14, a section of the story that she admits does not portray her in a flattering light. She starts to visit Nick frequently, sneaking to his room above the garage after her visits with the Commander. She tells Nick her real name and the details of the others—Moira and Ofglen. She keeps to herself only the details of Luke and of the message left by her predecessor. At the same time, she listens to Ofglen less and less, and tells her very little. She evades her queries and requests for information about the Commander.

At the Women's Salvaging (a public hanging where the audience actually touches the rope of the noose, thereby taking part in the execution), Ofglen and Offred watch the hanging of two Handmaids (one, Ofglen thinks, is Janine) and one Wife. Aunt Lydia officiates at the ceremony and announces that no formal sentence or explanation for the punishment will be read aloud. Offred can't bear to watch and looks at the grass as the stool is kicked from under the first Handmaid.

The public execution in chapter 42 is followed by a "Particicution" in chapter 43. A former Guardian is brought before the group. Ofglen drags Offred to the second row in the circle. At the whistle, the Handmaids, who have been told this Guardian is responsible for the rape of one of their own, are free to do with the prisoner as they choose. As they begin to rush forward, Offred hears him say, "I didn't . . ." (262), while Ofglen pushes him down and gives three hard kicks to his head. Offred is horrified until Ofglen tells her that he was one of theirs and that she knocked him out so he wouldn't feel himself being torn apart. As the crowd begins to thin, they notice Janine. Smeared with blood, she holds a clump of the Guardian's blond hair in her right hand and seems to have gone completely mad.

The next time Offred goes to meet Ofglen, there is a new Ofglen in her place. She uses the password, "Mayday," to determine whether or not this new Ofglen is a part of the network. She is not, but she clearly recognizes the word. Before the new Ofglen leaves she tells the narrator that her predecessor hung herself after the Salvaging, when she saw the van coming for her. A similar threat seems to await Offred when she returns home to find that Serena Joy knows about her night out with the Commander.

When the last night of the novel falls, in part 15, Offred is deep in thought about the options available to her: suicide, departure, a plea to Nick for help. She considers them all "idly" (274). However, before she can reach any decisions, the black van arrives. She is terrified until Nick enters the room and explains that the van is "Mayday." "Trust me," he tells her (275). Judging by the reaction of the Commander, who is concerned, and Serena Joy, who is furious, they have not been called by the household. However, as this section ends, the reader is unsure as to whether Offred is going to her death or not.

The 15 sections of the novel's narrative are followed by a section entitled "Historical Notes on *The Handmaid's Tale*." If one does not look closely, this seems to be a contextual document, the kind of critical commentary that might follow a novel in a critical edition of a classic work of literature. In fact, it is part of the novel itself. It declares itself to be a record of the details of an academic panel devoted to discussions of the Republic of Gilead at a historical convention, held at the University of Denay (deny?), Nunavit (none of it?), on June 25, 2195. This particular section describes a talk given by Professor Pioxoto from Cambridge University in England. Essentially, his talk reveals that the text may not be what Offred herself had intended. It is a transcription made, by Professor Pioxoto and Professor Wade, together with help from an "antiquarian technician," from cassette tapes found in an army trunk in Bangor, Maine. Professor Pioxoto acknowledges that the sequence of the narrative is largely due to their own editorial decisions. Further, the title comes from Professor Wade. Professor Pioxoto provides some contextual information for the Republic of Gilead, including the heightened rates of sterility that prompted its formation, the "President's Day Massacre" that caused the suspension of Congress thereby allowing the republic to emerge, and the purging of most of the first-wave or "early" Gilead Commanders that led to its demise. Pioxoto describes historians' inability to trace details either of the women or of those in the Mayday group. While he does offer two possible referents for the Commander himself, ultimately he is equally unsure about how Offred's story ends. His interest, however, lies not so much in uncovering whether she made it to safety but in figuring out how she managed to record the cassettes and how they arrived safely in Bangor. He concludes his talk by asking if there are any questions. For Atwood's readers, of course, his talk raises more questions than it answers. Highlighting again the fallibility and limitations of narrative, a theme that recurs throughout Offred's story, by asking if there are any questions, Atwood, through Pioxoto, is able to drive this point home. The reader is, of course, left with many questions, all of which will remain unanswered.

CHARACTER DEVELOPMENT

Offred is both the narrator of and the central character in her own story. Although she is also the heroine of the story, in the sense that she has romantic liaisons with a number of men and may even be rescued by one of them, she is far from heroic. Indeed, as the novel progresses, the reader sees her less as the victim of cruel circumstances than as someone who refused to act to change those circumstances when she had the chance. As Pioxoto reveals, her name, "Offred," is derived from that of her male guardian, the Commander Fred (Rooke 176). In part, perhaps, Atwood chose this name because it was not immediately obvious that it was a name composed from another name. However, the name "Offred" has other relevant connotations. Offred is praiseworthy in large part because she "offers" the stories of heroism that she witnesses, recording them for posterity. She, herself, is "afraid" (to play on a word that sounds like "Offred")—afraid to rally against the Revolution, to reveal herself to Ofglen, to spy on behalf of the Mayday group, to attempt escape, to commit suicide. Indeed, she seems afraid to act independently at all. The only risks she takes are either prompted by a male partner (the attempted escape from Gilead with Luke, her evening at Jezebel's with the Commander, and her eventual escape facilitated by Nick) or in order to be with a male partner (as in her nightly journeys to the Commander's office and later to Nick's bedroom). Consequently, she is not only "of Fred," but rather "of" or dependent upon a number of male partners. Fred is merely the partner designated her guardian by the Republic of Gilead. The final irony, of course, is that Offred is also "of" and offered by the two professors who transcribe her story and finally publish and comment upon it.

The most damning evidence against Offred emerges from her descriptions of the time "before." Although university educated, Offred's job was to transcribe books to disk form. As transcriber, she was a handmaid by profession. Further, she finds the Commander's comments about his wife being unable to understand him all too familiar because, after all, she has played the role of the other woman before as well, Luke having been married before he began his relationship with Offred. At these moments of revelation, Atwood's reader is forced to ponder whether things have really changed so dramatically for Offred in the postrevolutionary period.

Offred's behavior seems all the more passive because of the very active, even heroic, women around her. Offred's mother, Moira, and Ofglen are all punished (though, arguably, all choose their own fates rather than wait for punishment) for their outspoken resistance to Gilead, a fate that Offred seems to escape because of her unwillingness to speak out openly against the regime. Atwood's readers wonder, of course, whether Offred's contribution to the cause was valuable in any way. Most obviously, Offred's mother was a feminist activist in the pre-Gilead period, participating in demonstrations to eliminate pornography and support women's rights for abortion. Outspoken enough that she disappears from her apartment on the first day of the Revolution, Offred's mother is taken to the Colonies and appears on the film that Moira is shown when the "Eyes" finally capture her.

Moira is also heroic in her willingness to act quickly. When Janine has a nervous breakdown at the Red Centre, it is Moira who brings her back to her senses, quick to explain that hysteria will lead Janine to her death. It is Moira who ultimately escapes from the Red Centre, using her technical know-how to dismantle the toilet, and her courage and cunning to outwit the system. It is Moira who, when caught, opts to spend a few years at Jezebel's, where she can be open about her lesbian identity, rather than spend a longer time wasting away in the toxic filth of the Colonies.

By way of illustrating the possibility of heroism even within the ranks of the Handmaids, Atwood provides the example of Ofglen. Offred's shopping partner, Ofglen takes the risk of initiating conversation about the Mayday organization with Offred. She rushes to the aid of her comrade when he is presented to the Handmaids at the Particicution as a rapist, giving him a series of hard kicks in a gesture of mercy that may, indeed, have cost Ofglen her own life. It is, after all, immediately after the Particicution that the black van arrives at her doorstep. She, however, is quick to act and commits suicide. Her behavior stands in marked contrast to Offred's when the black van arrives at her own doorstep.

The more secondary female characters share, with Offred, responsibility for their participation in the regime and, consequently, for their own fate.

Serena Joy, a gospel singer and preacher from before, was unwittingly one of the spokespeople for the regime. Professor Pioxoto identifies historical models for Serena Joy in the wives of the two possible historical referents for the Commander. One was named "Thelma," the other "Bambi Fae." Combined, their names remind Atwood's readers of Tammy Faye Baker, the famous gospel singer who, with her husband Jim Baker, suffered a change of lifestyle when the illegal practices of their charitable foundation were exposed. Many readers would have recognized this allusion to Tammy Faye in the description of Serena Joy's blond hair and in Offred's memory of Serena Joy's running mascara in her emotional television performances.

Other women who are clearly guilty for their complicity with the system are the Aunts. As Pioxoto explains, these women might have become Aunts due to either their agreement with the "traditional values" of the system or, more simply, due to a desire for self-preservation along with some power and benefits. To signal their allegiance with the system, Atwood provides them with names derived from commercial household products. They, like their namesakes (Elizabeth Arden, Betty Crocker, etc.), are spokespersons for the system.

Janine provides a more ambiguous example of a woman who tries to comply with the system. At the Red Centre, where she makes frequent confessions about her past behavior in front of the other Handmaids; in her later placements, as she conceives children with her doctor so as to fulfill her procreative duty; and in the Particicution, where the blond hair in her hands after the event suggests she did, indeed, participate actively, Janine attempts to do what is expected of her. Ultimately, though, it breaks her.

The fates of all these women—passive and active—illustrate the ironies inherent in the Republic of Gilead. Although Gilead was a society developed to protect women, Atwood's readers must wonder just which women it protects and what kind of protection it provides.

Generally, the male characters in this novel are not well developed. This is not so much an oversight on Atwood's part as it is a strategy to focus on women's stories and experience in a society dominated in very obvious ways by men. It is ironic, therefore, that we know so much more about Offred's way of thinking by the end of the novel than we know about "Fred's," even though we never gain access to such basic details as her name. Further, even though readers come to know Commander Fred better than the other men in the novel, what they come to know are the inconsistencies he embodies. Although, for example, he is one of the key leaders of the regime, he is curiously uncomfortable with some aspects of it. He has kept magazines from pre-Gilead days, for example, even though the regime requires their destruction. He condones, even frequents, "Jezebel's," a nightclub reminiscent of pre-Gilead times, even though such sexual license supposedly has been eliminated in Gilead. More generally, he seems disappointed with Gilead, a disappointment that is mirrored in his own personal life. Certainly his own marriage to Serena Joy seems very unsatisfying to him. With Offred, he relishes the simple pleasures of a game of Scrabble with an opponent whose skills leave open the possibility that she can beat him.

The other male characters in the novel also seem to be divided in their loyalty to and challenge of the regime. As such, Offred's guardians provide her with a precarious sense of security. This holds true for such minor characters as Offred's doctor, who defies the regime by offering to impregnate her. It also holds true for Offred's partners. Her husband Luke, for example, seemed curiously happy when Offred first finds herself without access to her own bank accounts and begins to spend more time at home instead of going out to work each day. However, it is also Luke who ultimately decides to risk escaping so as to find a better life for her, a risk that ultimately costs him his life.

Nick, too, works simultaneously within and against the system. He is the Commander's driver, so loyal that he complies with Serena Joy's request that he sleep with Offred so as to give the Commander a child. Offred, however, feels that his behavior reveals not loyalty but daring resistance. Even before Serena Joy requests that he sleep with Offred, he has eyed her as she walks by, flirting as much as might be possible under the circumstances. Further, at the novel's end, Nick goes well beyond the request of Serena Joy to become Offred's lover and, possibly, as a result of his working relationship with the resistance movement, becomes her rescuer. Given that readers never hear from Nick himself, his motives remain ambiguous.

However, the male guardian who provides the most precarious security of all is one in whose hands Offred ultimately places not so much her life as her life story. Ironically, the most fully developed character in the novel is that of Professor Pioxoto who, technically, plays no role *in* Offred's narrative itself. His misogyny (or hatred and dismissal of the value of women) is evident in a number of crude jokes peppered throughout his paper. He begins his paper with a comment about the panel coordinator, Professor Maryann Crescent Moon, explaining his enjoyment of the Artic char fish dish the evening before and his present enjoyment of the "Arctic

Chair," where the word "enjoy" might be understood in "two distinct senses," though not in the "obsolete third" (282). Is he implying that Professor Crescent Moon is too old to be sexually attractive? Is he implying that he "enjoyed" her, in the past tense, but "enjoys" her no longer? Either way, the insinuation is an insult to his professional colleague. He notes, for example, that Professor Wade intended a pun on the word "tail," (a derogatory term for women's sexual attractiveness) when he selected the title of "The Handmaid's Tale" (283). He describes "The Underground Femaleroad" (Moira's means of escape and a phrase that itself plays on the "Underground Railroad") as the "Underground Frailroad" (283). Taken together, these barbs suggest that men's attitudes toward women are dismissive and hostile in the year 2195. The Republic of Gilead, and the various arguments for women's rights contained within Offred's narratives, do not seem to have had much impact on Professor Pioxoto for one.

NARRATIVE STRUCTURE

Atwood's *The Handmaid's Tale* consists of two parts: the tale itself and a section entitled "Historical Notes on *The Handmaid's Tale*." Offred's "tale" consists of 15 parts, essentially tracing Offred's daily routines and alternating between night and day. Offred's narrative begins and ends with "Night," signaling the darkness that has descended upon Offred's life. There is one exception to this pattern. The day in which we see Offred participate in the first "Ceremony," or ritual copulation with the Commander, is described over the course of four parts (parts 4–7). Here, part 5 is entitled "Nap" rather than "Night." However, the nightmarish dreams it describes are equally as bleak as those found in the other "Night" sections.

In addition, Atwood provides a "Historical Notes" section, in which a fictional professor in the year 2195 analyzes Offred's text in various "historical" contexts. Ironically, then, these *historical* notes prompt Atwood's reader to compare Offred's narrative, itself set in our speculative future, with a fictional future. By contrast, the first epigraph to the novel, which establishes the precedent of Gilead in Rachel's suggestion that Jacob have her child by her handmaid Bilhah (Genesis 30: 1–3), invites readers to compare Offred's narrative with the biblical past. Inevitably, Atwood's reader must conclude that not much has changed.

Offred narrates her own story in the present tense. This serves to heighten suspense. For example, when Offred ventures into Serena Joy's parlor one night and is startled by Nick, we, as readers, are startled along with her. When the black van pulls up outside the Commander's house, we are relieved, along with Offred, to hear that it is Mayday rather than the terrifying "Eyes" who have come for her. Consequently, the present-tense narration serves to elicit our sympathy for Offred, since we share her reactions as she describes the various challenges of her situation. Without the immediacy of this narrative technique, readers might be far more judgmental of Offred's hesitance, her refusal to act and make decisions quickly.

THEMES AND ALLUSIONS

In this novel about who can control whom and set in the Republic of Gilead, a society where the distribution of information is strictly controlled, words and names become powerful weapons. Prayers are printed by the state in various "Soul Scrolls" facilities, and then distributed to the individual households. Television news, judging by the episode Offred watches before the Ceremony, provides carefully censored reports, as in Orwell's *1984*. Even the public executions provide virtually no information about the nature of the crime that warrants public hanging. Consequently, the most precious gift that the Commander can give Offred is access to printed material, to the books on his shelves and the magazines in his drawers. In turn, what he most wants is precisely what he can no longer have easily in a society without books: an engaging discussion or game of words, like Scrabble. Perhaps conversation is the "balm" or source of health for Gilead. The term itself is comes from an image used by God (Jeremiah 8:22) when he asks why his people have not followed him. "Is there no balm in Gilead?" he asks, "no physician there?"

Even in her games of Scrabble, Offred is concerned about who wins the game and how. She is proud, for example, to win the first game over the Commander. Only later, when they come to know one another, does she realize that he let her win that first game. He had controlled the board all along. That victory is a small one, but indicative of the Commander's role more generally. After all, as Offred knows, the one who can control the story can also control the story's ending. In the Republic of Gilead, Offred clearly does not control the narrative. The original script comes from the Bible (its source, Genesis 30:1–3, is quoted in the novel's first epigraph), and the "early Commanders" (to use Pioxoto's terms) developed this slim script into a full-length production, complete with costumes and props. In the grand scheme of things, Offred has just a bit part. In her own narrative, however, Offred plays the most important roles: protagonist and narrator. Again and again, she describes what she is doing as a story, by way of exerting her control over what happens in it and who hears it. Ironically, however, her actions, dependent as they are on what those around her tell her to do, suggest that, in reality, she has very little say in what happens. Moreover, in the Historical Notes section at the end of Atwood's book, it becomes clear that this is not Offred's story at all. Rather, it is a story reconstructed by Professors Pioxoto and Wade. In the war of words, Offred has lost.

Other forms of communication are important in the narrative as well. In a society with ritualized sexual intercourse, hangings, and beatings, intimate touch is a precious commodity. The Commander and Offred never kiss during the Ceremony. Consequently, when alone in the hotel room, it is the gentle touch and kiss that the Commander craves most. Similarly, eye contact proves to be a very powerful indicator of an individual's allegiances. Seldom will Offred raise her head to meet the eyes of the individuals to whom she speaks. This is partially because of the way her uniform is made. As a Handmaid, her head flanked by the white wings of her uniform, she must actually raise her head and turn it toward another individual to meet his or her eyes directly. Further Handmaids are trained to keep their eyes demurely turned down. Notably, Moira's transformation into an Aunt consists of her changing her posture as well as her costume (124). However, refusing to meet an individual's gaze is also a question of control on Offred's part. When Nick first winks at Offred, she lowers her head quickly (18). When the Guardians watch her walk, shopping basket in hand, she moves her hips but never looks up (22). It is no coincidence that the most frightening members of this regime are the "Eyes," those who see all, as the eye painted on their black van emphasizes, but whose own activities are not fully understood.

A related theme in this novel is that of secrecy. In a world where identities are regimented, behavior monitored, and interaction dictated, moments of privacy are rare and precious. What Offred comes to understand is that even as she and Luke found things so unbearable that they risked flight, they were still happy. Hidden in Offred's narrative, so hidden that they can reach beyond and through the reconstruction of her narrative, are signs of humanity's real treasure: human intimacy. Offred reveals her name to Nick by way of giving him her most precious possession. She may, indeed, provide us with enough hints so that her most attentive listeners can hear it as well. So, too, does Atwood leave a sign of her own presence in the text, of her vote of support for the value of human relationships. Carved in a desktop at the Red Centre, the pencil having in-scribed it "many times," Offred finds the inscription: "M. loves G., 1972" (107). Nineteen seventy-two was the first of many happy years in Mar-garet Atwood's relationship to her partner Graeme Gibson.

A READER-RESPONSE INTERPRETATION

Reader-response criticism, which focused on the reader's role in pro-ducing the meaning of a text, was largely a phenomenon of the late 1960s and 1970s. It was a reaction to New Criticism (see the "thematic reading" section in the chapter on *Cat's Eye* in this study) and its insistence on interpreting the text independently from the context of its production (the author or her environment) or reception (the reader and her environment) (Schellenberg 170). Reader-response theorists describe a variety of differ-ent readers, ranging from the "actual" or "real" reader, whose reading abilities correspond to the average educated general reader, to the "ideal" reader, whose reading abilities exceed those of the typical general reader. These theorists' interpretations, however, all share an emphasis on the way meaning unfolds as the reader makes his or her way through the text. Indeed, reader-response analyses see the meaning of a text as being con-structed not only by the author but also by the reader. As such, reader-response critics see a literary text not so much a finished product but rather as something that is developed with each new reading. In turn, the reader-response critic has the responsibility of describing how a reader goes about "making sense" of that literary text. Hence, for example, a reader-response analysis of a Shakespearean play might discuss the ex-perience of twentieth-century readers as they gain familiarity with Shake-spearean language and the context of Shakespeare's time, as well as the evolution of their understanding of Shakespeare's play.

In the case of *The Handmaid's Tale*, there seem to be at least four stages to the reading process, if (and this is not always the case with "real" readers approaching the novel for the first time) the reader recognizes the "Historical Notes" section to be a part of the novel.

Four Stages of the Reading Process

The first stage of reading is directed by the novel's epigraphs: a passage from Genesis outlining the Biblical origin of the notion of a handmaid; a quote from Jonathan Swift; and a Sufi proverb. If the Biblical passage provides historical precedent for the novel's futuristic society, and the Sufi proverb underlines the lunacy possible when lawmakers lose sight of common sense, then the quote from Swift signals that the novel we are about to read is a satire. Taken from the opening of Swift's famous "A Modest Proposal," the passage does not describe the "modest" proposal itself: the monstrous idea that the impoverished and hungry Irish look to their own babies as the source of food and, through sale as such, as the source of income. Rather, it describes the rationale for that "modest proposal": a visionary thought that is the opposite of "vain" or "idle," in other words, one that is useful and practical. Of course, his proposal *is* practical. It is also inhumane and violates Western society's greatest taboo: cannibalism. The vile disregard for the sanctity of human life displayed by Swift's speaker in this memorable work proves to be an exaggeration of what Swift perceives to be the general tone of the British attitude toward the suffering Irish. Swift, as a satirist, exaggerates to prove his point. Satire is built on irony: the gap between what the author says, through his speaker in the case of Swift's proposal, and what he means. As a result of this epigraph from Swift, then, we brace ourselves to read a satiric novel, one that is going to present a "modest proposal," a practical concept that will be an exaggerated form of some of the distasteful attitudes in our society.

Satire is exactly what we find as we begin reading the novel and enter the second stage of the reading process. Gilead's "practical" solution to the ills of its society (which are, not coincidentally, the ills of our own society)—pollution and its resulting infertility, crime, and the disintegration of personal relationships—is regimented behavior. Of course, what Commander Fred and presumably the other commanders of the early Gilead regime seem to perceive as a solution is what Offred and we, as Atwood's readers, see as a nightmarish problem. The irony, or distance between the official account of Gilead and what we understand from it, is apparent.

A third reading emerges when Offred's nightmare is transformed somewhat, toward the end of the novel as she simultaneously develops a relationship with two different men: the Commander and Nick. As Stephanie Barbé Hammer notes, at this point the novel begins to read like a popular gothic romance, "for in such stories the heroine, like Offred, is often made a helpless prisoner by an evil and sexually desirous male force, until she is finally liberated by the romantic hero" (41).

The fourth and final stage of the reading comes when Professor Pioxoto reveals that the absorbing story we have just read—and the woman we have come to know so well—is largely a fictional construct. Even worse,

her author is a man of distasteful opinions, including the very same mi-
sogynistic attitudes that had plagued Offred in Gilead.

Locating the Targets of Satire

Satire always has a "butt" or target. In the case of Atwood's novel,
however, there are a number of different targets, a new one emerging with
each stage of the reading process. At first glance, the target is clearly radical Christian fundamentalism of the kind found in North America during
the early 1980s. However, the novel itself provides some more specific
answers to the question, Who is really to blame for the mess?

Like Offred, our first reaction is to blame the Commanders. Did they
not forget to take account of the human need for love and the warmth of
human relationships in their plan for an ideal society? As with the "modest proposal" of Swift's speaker, their vision was inhumane. However, as
the satire unfolds, Offred soon realizes that they are not the only ones to
blame; a number of women could also be held responsible. After all, both
her mother and Serena Joy had wanted a women's society. Gilead isn't
quite what they imagined, but it is a society designed to protect (certain)
women. Further, Gilead's existence depends upon the cooperation of female enforcers, namely the Aunts. Indeed, Gilead is not a technological
society that relies upon advanced weaponry for law enforcement. (The
cattle prods, for instance, are positively archaic). As in the Holocaust of
WWII, Gilead co-opts some of its citizens to patrol others—either as spies
(or Eyes), as Aunts, or as participants in the various ceremonies of execution and ritual beating. That the Aunts have names derived from
domestic-product spokespersons, however, is a subtle indication that
their role in Gilead is not so different from the role of the corporate
spokesperson in our own day: to perpetuate conformity.

When the narrative takes a turn toward gothic romance, Atwood's
reader starts the feel that Offred, too, should perhaps shoulder some responsibility for Gilead. Surely her willingness to serve the Commander
as a Handmaid is not fundamentally much different from her role as
Luke's handmaid in the time before. Then, as now, she followed the lead
of the men around her. Then, as now, she refused to act out or speak up
against the regime out of fear for her own safety.

However, our sympathy for Offred and the plight of all handmaids is
revived during the fourth stage in the reading process. Here, we see another target of Atwood's satire: the officious male critics of the "Historical
Notes" section. Even in 2195, they continue to exercise censorship by pay-

ing more attention to the Commander's identity than to Offred's own story. Rather than learn from the story, Professors Wade and Pioxoto merely reconstruct it. And, although the power structure has shifted somewhat in the years between the Gileadean regime and 2195—the chair of the conference is an Inuit woman—the male academics still make remarks that patronize women and go uncensored (indeed, are even applauded) by the audience.

All these shortcomings—human fear and passivity, blindness about the real value of human relationships, and the willingness to patronize others and tolerate double standards—are, of course, elements of our own time as well. As soon as we recognize this, we, as Atwood's readers, find ourselves in the uncomfortable position of being the butt of a very pointed satire. Despite this, the book has engaged rather than distanced real audiences. *The Handmaid's Tale* was on the *New York Times* best-seller list for 23 weeks, and it cemented Atwood's reputation on the international literary scene, breaking the sound barrier in terms of mainstream popularity for her work. As a result, Atwood is widely recognized as one of the leading satirists of the twentieth century, central to a Tradition (even now) dominated by men.

8

The Blind Assassin
(2000)

We have traced the way Atwood's novels reverse expectations about character, as in the artist novels where the woman becomes the artist rather than the model, and setting, as in the speculative and dystopian fiction. In this chapter, we turn to the way Atwood reverses our expectations about plot. In the villainess novels (*The Robber Bride*, *Alias Grace*, and *Blind Assassin*), Atwood forces us to question some basic assumptions about the nature of villainy in fiction: first, that villains are not the sympathetic first-person narrators and central protagonists of literary works, and second, that villains, especially those who commit crimes against women, are usually men.

Early signs of such challenges appear in *Cat's Eye*, which serves as a kind of bridge between the artist novels and the villainess novels. After all, there is something decidedly frightening to Elaine about the little group of girls she calls friends and especially about their ringleader, Cordelia. Yet, does it not seem unusual for villains to come in such small and female packages? What is particularly deceptive about Cordelia is that she is both victim and victimizer. In the case of Cordelia's victimization of Elaine, those roles are played sequentially. We watch her fall from a position of authority, in which she serves as the leader of the group of girls who taunt Elaine, to a position of vulnerability as she becomes an increasingly unhappy and dysfunctional adult.

However, in the "villainess" novels, the central character or villainess is simultaneously powerful and powerless, at the same time terrifying and engaging her readers. Examples of Atwood's fascinating villainesses include: Xenia who, as the heroine of *The Robber Bride*, is a female version of the Grimms' gruesome robber bridegroom (from the fairy tale of the same name); Grace Marks, the heroine and alleged murderess of Atwood's play *The Servant Girl* and of her novel *Alias Grace*, whose character treads the fine line between innocent servant girl (the character called Grace Marks) and her more violent alter ego, Mary Whitney. The most recent villainess of Atwood's novels is Iris Griffen, one of the blind assassins in the novel of that name. We will focus at length on this novel as an example of the villainess series both because the book has so far received little in-depth commentary and because Iris is a wonderful example of how one character can be so steeped in the rank darkness of villainy and self-deception and still appear so beguilingly sympathetic.

PLOT DEVELOPMENT

Divided into 15 parts, the novel incorporates a number of different kinds of writing: newspaper clippings; sections of a novel itself called *The Blind Assassin* (which, like *Lady Oracle*, is a book within a book); descriptions of photographs and images; as well as the reminiscences of an elderly woman (Mrs. Iris Griffen), who explains that she is compiling the story of her life for her granddaughter. Part 1 of the novel introduces the two dominant lines of narrative: the story of a family dynasty and the novel within Atwood's novel of the same name. The connection between these two lines of narrative is largely unclear, except that the same character figures in both. Laura Chase is the victim of a car accident, described in the novel's first section in the form of an article clipped from the *Toronto Star*. She seems also to be the author of the embedded novel, *The Blind Assassin*, published in New York in 1947, a section of which is excerpted in the third section of part 1. Consequently, the novel's introduction establishes suspense—What caused Laura Chase's fateful dive off the bridge?—and invites its readers to become detectives to establish the precise relationship between Laura Chase's book and her subsequent death. Readers rightly presume that the answers will emerge as Iris Griffen, Laura's sister, unravels her story.

Part 1 also introduces an important piece of evidence that will serve as a clue for readers in their investigation of the novel's mysteries and will reappear at regular intervals to signal significant developments in readers' understanding of events. This clue is a photograph of three individuals sitting under an apple tree. The word "picnic" is written in pencil on the back side. In this first mention of the photograph, it seems to be an object treasured by the woman in Laura Chase's novel because it provides one of the last traces of her lost lover. Curiously, there is a disembodied hand at the edge of the photo. This last detail is provided in part 1 but never fully explained until the photograph's final appearance in part 15. That is, the relationship of the photograph to the novel's title and central image becomes clear only toward the end of the novel when readers understand that the disembodied hand figuratively belongs to Iris Griffen, this novel's titular blind assassin.

The notion of blind assassin is also introduced very early in the novel. In the sections of part 2 devoted to excerpts from Chase's novel, *Blind Assassin*, we overhear the story told by a fugitive male lover (presumably the lover captured in the "picnic" photograph) to his girlfriend about the planet Zycron and its five warring tribes. He talks about the slave children who are forced to weave intricate carpets, work that ultimately forces them to go blind. Once blind, they are sold to brothels, but some become assassins.

These young men are not the only blind assassins in Atwood's novel. Even in the novel's earliest pages, we realize that the Chase and Griffen dynasties have suffered a number of tragedies. Most obviously, the four newspaper clippings in part 2 describe three different deaths, those of Richard Griffen in 1947; Aimee Griffen, of a broken neck in 1975, after years of alcohol and drug abuse; and Winifred Griffen Prior in 1998 at age 92. In none of these clippings is there mention of "foul play." However, as the novel unfolds, it becomes clear to Atwood's readers that none of these deaths—nor, indeed, the death of Iris's father, Norval—was entirely without foul play. These individuals were not murdered. But they were certainly pushed to the brink of self-assassination by the various blind assassins of Atwood's novel.

Who are these blind assassins? To reveal the full extent of the answer here is to take away the genuine suspense and intrigue of the novel, which is carefully plotted at the level of minute detail. However, it is helpful to think of this novel as having three sections, each one comprised of five "parts," as the novel's 15 units are called, with parts 5 and 10 serving as sectional transitions. This tripartite model is especially helpful to understand the development of Iris's narrative of her life. Parts 1 through 5, for example, describe the Chase family dynasty from the perspective of the elderly Iris, née Chase. Richard Griffen is introduced in part 4, where the eight sections move back and forth between a description of the mighty beginning to the fall, in the story of Chase Industries during the Depression of the 1930s, and the gradual empowerment of the disempowered, in the man's story of the blind assassins in Zycron. Next, parts 5 through 10 reveal the eclipse of the Chase dynasty by the Griffen dynasty at the hand of Iris's husband, Richard Griffen, and his partner in crime, sister Winifred. Finally, parts 10 through 15 outline the demise of the Griffens at the hand of Iris herself. In other words, the three sections of the novel are dominated by three different blind assassins: those described in the story told by the male fugitive of Laura Chase's novel, *The Blind Assassin*; Richard Griffen; and Iris.

That image of "the hand" reappears, of course, every time readers catch a new glimpse of the "picnic" photo with its disembodied hand. Indeed, the photo's reappearance in each of the novel's three sections emphasizes this particular tripartite structure. At first mention of the photo, in part 1, Atwood's readers cannot be sure whose hand they are seeing. After all, the photo is far removed from Iris's narrative, since it is held by a character in Laura Chase's novel. In this first section of Atwood's novel, the blind assassins also seem far removed from Iris, since they too figure as characters in Laura's novel.

When the scene of the photo reappears in part 5, readers come to understand that the three people figured in it are Laura and Iris, at the 1934 Chase and Sons Labor Day Celebration picnic hosted by their father and his button company, as well as Alex Thomas, a former student of divinity. Not only do readers link this moment with the scene captured in the photograph in the novel within this novel, *The Blind Assassin*, but also they assume Laura and Alex to be the couple in the original photograph entitled "picnic." Further, they understand the reasons behind the story-teller's fugitive status to be his involvement in the union-inspired riot and the resulting fire and death of the night watchman, which contributed to the demise of the Chase Button Factory. The photo of the two girls sitting with Alex under the apple tree is published in the local newspaper the day after the picnic. When Laura later works for the newspaper, she steals the negative and makes two prints of it. After Alex Thomas's departure from their home, where they have harbored him from the authorities following the riot, Laura presents Iris with one of the pictures she has of the three of them, with her cut out of it, and keeps one for herself with Iris cut out of it. Only the hand of the other sister is visible in each photo. This detail further explains the appearance of a hand at the side of the photo.

More generally, photographs function in this novel as messages, in a language spoken largely by Laura to her sister. In part 11, a section foreshadowing further revelations of Richard's villainy as well as Iris's inability to see and stop it in time, Laura leaves a message for her sister by tinting some of the photographs in Iris's wedding album. In the formal photo of the bride and groom, Richard's face is a dark gray and he is tinted red, with flames appearing behind him. Iris has been bleached to look blurred.

If the tripartite structure of the novel is emphasized by the reappearance of photos, it is underlined in another way as well. With the introduction of each new section, Atwood's readers are invited to reconsider Laura's death. At first it appears to be an accident (part 1), next a possible suicide (part 5), and, finally, almost a murder (at the hands of Richard in part 10 and at the hands of Iris in part 14). In part 1, for example, the car's plummet off the bridge into a ravine seems to have been caused by streetcar tracks, even though some observers noted that Laura seemed to steer the car off the bridge. In part 5, Iris recalls the way in which Laura, then age six, jumped into a river near their home and almost drowned soon after their mother died of a miscarriage. Although little comes of this incident, it does indicate Laura's willfulness and serves to foreshadow the possibility that Laura's eventual death was a suicide rather than an accident.

One other incident in their childhood foreshadows Laura's future. She claims that her tutor, Mr. Erskine, puts his hand in her shirt and under her skirt, but Iris isn't sure she believes her. Luckily for Laura, their housekeeper, Reenie, does believe her and manages to plant some incriminating evidence such that he is promptly fired. Although this incident is quickly resolved, the next time Laura is inappropriately approached by a man—this time Iris's husband and Laura's brother-in-law, Richard—the consequences will be dire. Once again, Iris will not take Laura's side quickly enough, and this time Reenie will not have the power to alter the tragic sequence of events. Only after Laura's death, in fact, will Iris understand the implications of the notebooks she leaves in Iris's top drawer: that the marks of "x" and "o" indicate the days when Richard had sex with Laura aboard the yacht *The Water Nixie*.

In the central section of the novel, that is, Richard Griffen is clearly the villain. In part 7, approximately the novel's central point, the threat posed by Richard Griffen becomes explicit. After Iris's marriage to him and Laura's attempted escape from him, Laura confesses to Iris that she feels trapped and in danger. This confession is similar to her earlier announcement about Mr. Erskine's behavior toward her. Iris tries to soothe her, but realizes that she has been naïve. Living with Richard could, indeed, be dangerous, as could associating with his treacherous sister, Winifred.

The rest of this section tells the story of the treachery of the men in the Chase sisters' lives. Alex, whom we suspect of harboring ill will toward the Chase family because of its capitalist philosophy, appears in the "Xanadu" section. What we discover, however, is that Alex's deception has to do with maintaining a relationship with both, rather than only one, of the Chase sisters. As Iris dresses for the party, donning her costume as the Abyssinian maid (who plays her dulcimer and sings of Mount Abora in Samuel Taylor Coleridge's famous poem "Kubla Khan"), Laura confesses to having seen Alex in Toronto. As readers, however, we learn in the section entitled "Besotted" (a word that, later in the novel, takes on significance in relation to Richard's inappropriate attraction for Laura) that Iris has also seen Alex Thomas. We know little of what happens after their encounter, but Iris thinks that, at the moment she stretched her hand to him, she had "committed treachery" in her heart (321). Does she commit treachery again when she says nothing of this to Laura? At this halfway point in the novel, then, readers begin to suspect and investigate Iris more closely. Indeed, some may notice that the woman in Laura Chase's novel is dressed, in part 6, in a way that seems more typical for Iris than for her sister, Laura, whom they earlier assumed to be the character in Laura Chase's novel.

However, readers are not meant to be suspicious of all the characters in Atwood's novel. One family—that of the Chase family housekeeper, Reenie, and particularly her daughter, Myra, and son-in-law, Walter— proves to be a beacon of sound judgment and generosity. Laura, the only other character untainted by deception, frequently turns to Reenie for help. After the deaths of Reenie and Laura, it is Walter and Myra who always appear when Iris needs a lift, a hand with the snow shovel, or a moral boost. Indeed, Walter's behavior stands in stark contrast to that of the other men in Iris's life at the center point of the novel. It is here that we learn of the death of Iris's father, who has died, alone, distraught, and probably drunk, in a garret of his home. It is also here that we see Richard Griffen stoop to withhold from his wife the news of her father's death until it is far too late for her to attend his funeral or to comfort her sister. Walter's constant presence, straightforwardness, and generosity to Iris is striking, then, when contrasted with her father's habit of absenting himself when difficulty strikes (his whereabouts when his wife had a miscarriage are shrouded in mystery), with Richard's devious manipulation, and even with Alex Thomas's behavior. Skipping ahead to part 10, one cannot help but notice that this other man in Iris's and Laura's life, Alex Thomas, seems to absent himself as well. When, in part 10, the woman of Chase's novel looks through a copy of *The Lizard Men of the Planet Xenor,* a novel written by the male lover and based on the story told between the two lovers, she is disappointed to find only lizard men in the story and no trace of either the love story they had developed together or of a message for her.

Also, at the center point of the novel, the two dominant lines of narrative begin to converge. In part 8, the female character in Laura Chase's novel announces that she will be gone for a month on a ship's maiden voyage. Although it promises to be the social event of the century and her attendance is required, she explains that she does not want to go. Immediately following this discussion, Atwood provides a clipping from *Mayfair* of July 1936 describing the maiden voyage the *Queen Mary.* Iris and Richard are on this voyage as part of their honeymoon trip. Among the outfits described in the article was a chiffon cape trimmed with ermine tails that is most likely Iris's. Here, then, Atwood's readers must wonder whether the woman in Laura Chase's *The Blind Assassin* is Iris, rather than Laura.

That is, if at the novel's center point readers see deception in most of the male characters, then in the last section of the novel they begin to view Iris with suspicion. Parts 10 through 15 develop the story of Iris's complicity in the web of deception that ultimately brought tragedy to the two family dynasties of which she was a member. The last third of the novel opens with reference to Iris's persistent nightmares, signaling a deep-seated anxiety. Early in her marriage, a doctor diagnosed her difficulty as having to do with her "conscience" (372). But what is this seemingly frail, elderly woman guilty of? Until this point, she and her sister seem to be victims of Richard Griffen's plan to bring the Chase family to its knees. The answer, developed in the novel's third section, is that Iris is guilty of a great deal. At the very least, she has proved to be a poor guardian and parent. At most, she is a murderer.

First, Iris has been an unhelpful guardian and mentor both to her younger sister, Laura (who suffers abuse at the hands of Iris's husband, is impregnated by him, and is subsequently silenced by incarceration in an insane asylum), and to her own daughter, Aimee (who is removed to Winifred's guardianship). Certainly, too, Iris has served as accomplice to Richard's villainy; just as wartime allies must bear the responsibility for their actions, so must Iris bear responsibility for Richard's actions. In part 7, details of war are themselves a version of the story—this one about the way individuals treat one another. Richard Griffen's support for authority, here articulated in his support of the Munich Accord and of a strong Germany, as cited in an October 7, 1938, *Globe and Mail* entry, parallels his dealings with his own family, especially his wife and her sister. His stated philosophy about the Munich Accord—that prosperity will erase the pain of the previous difficult years—might apply equally well to the rationale for his treatment of the Chase family.

Part 13, however, provides evidence that Iris is far more than a mere accomplice to the crime. The opening sections foreshadow the dramatic conclusion of part 13 by expanding upon the parallel between wartime conditions and the Chase-Griffen family drama. As the elderly Iris watches the news from her home in Port Ticonderoga, and as she remembers hearing about the start of WWII when Richard hastily switched his allegiances from Germany to Russia, she thinks that most elderly people would like to watch the end of the world from a distant and detached place. The implication is that Iris cannot have this comfortable distance, and precisely why she cannot is revealed in the novel's final chapters that provide evidence of Iris's role in the deaths of both her husband and her sister.

First, we learn that Richard Griffen shot himself. Upon publication of Laura's book, the rumor that Laura committed suicide, hushed at the time of her death, resurfaces and kills Richard's chances of political leadership. Further, an anonymous tip (presumably from Iris) is made about Laura's incarceration at the rehabilitation center, Bella Vista, which prompts an investigation. Understanding that Iris has finally trumped him, Richard commits suicide with a copy of *The Blind Assassin* beside him. Presumably, he thought the female character in Laura's novel was Laura herself and that the novel provided evidence of Laura's affair with Alex Thomas.

The next clue about Iris's guilt surfaces when we learn that Laura's death follows a conversation with Iris in which the latter reveals news of Alex Thomas's death and of her own longstanding love affair with him. At the news, Laura's reaction of shock is immediate. She wears the same expression she had on the day Iris pulled her out of the river after her mother's death, the day she almost drowned.

Finally, and most significantly, readers' suspicion that Iris herself penned, and presumably "starred" in, the novel attributed to Laura Chase is confirmed by Iris herself. In part 14, readers return to the events that opened the novel: those surrounding Laura's death. Here, though, readers glimpse those events through Iris's eyes as she learns of the death and prepares to go to the morgue to identify the body. She opens her glove drawer to find the notebooks that we have all along assumed contained the manuscript for Laura's novel. Instead of a manuscript, however, the drawer contains Laura's notes: including a translation from Latin of the final scene from Virgil's *Aeneid,* in which one character is significantly named Iris, and a mathematics notebook containing a list of dates, with either the word "no" or an "x" and, in one case, an "o" jotted next to each date. These cryptic markings, Iris realizes, indicate the days on which Richard had sexual relations with Laura against her will.

In such a twice-told tale as this novel, it is perhaps not surprising that the details of Iris's last thoughts—as she sits daydreaming in her garden just before her death, thinking about handing her manuscript over to her granddaughter—appear after we have read her obituary in the *Port Ticon-deroga Herald* of May 29, 1999. Also unsurprising is how little the obituary really captures the woman we have come to know as Iris. How peaceful was Iris, we wonder, during those last days? Her nightmares, together with the acknowledgment in part 15 that the "picnic" photograph captured a moment of happiness in a lifetime of unhappiness, suggest that she was not at all at peace with herself or her actions.

CHARACTER DEVELOPMENT

Iris plays the role of villainess in this novel. As such, she is not to be confused with the more two-dimensional monsters played by the two Griffen siblings. Winifred, in her single-minded antagonism toward Iris, is typical of Atwood's gorgon figures. Gorgons stem from Greek mythology and are "three mythical female personages, with snakes for hair, whose look turned the beholder into stone. The one of most note, and the only one mortal, Medusa, was slain by Perseus, and her head fixed on Athene's shield" ("gorgon"). Other examples in Atwood's novels include Aunt Muriel in *Life before Man* and Joan's horrible mother in *Lady Oracle.* At certain moments, Mrs. Smeath of *Cat's Eye* qualifies for the role as well, not to mention the landlady in *The Edible Woman.* In her poem "The Landlady" from *The Animals in That Country,* we catch a small glimpse of one other such figure. What distinguishes the gorgon from the villainess is the lack of ambivalence in her character portrayal. Winifred may be complex, embodying both the genteel and civilized public persona and the ruthlessly determined private one, but she is ultimately a flat and two-dimensional character.

Richard Griffen is equally two-dimensional, something that Iris acknowledges in a moment that reads like Atwood's own response to similar criticism of her earlier work (from critics like Brophy, Elliott, Fraser, and Skelton, for example). From his entrance onto the stage during the Chase and Sons Labor Day picnic onward, he shows himself to be the consummate con artist always intent on self-advancement and able to convince Norval Chase, the media, and frequently Iris herself to see things his way. Laura is the one person who is always beyond the reach of his persuasion. If he is never able to persuade her, however, he does succeed in silencing her.

Alex Thomas, the other central male character, is cast in the role of the romantic hero, albeit a rather ineffectual one. He seems all the more virtuous because he is a character foil to Richard Griffen. Whereas Griffen is wealthy, Alex, an ex-divinity student, is impoverished. Whereas Griffen is a capitalist and a political conservative, Alex is committed to socialist causes. Whereas Griffen seeks to expose Alex, using Callista as an informant, and to usurp his relationship with, it seems, both Chase girls, Alex seems to spend his time hiding, first at the Chase home and perhaps later in the various apartments described in Chase's *The Blind Assassin*. Whereas the romantic hero would normally confront and defeat the villain, however, that moment never occurs. Alex dies at war and leaves Laura and Iris to take on the monster alone.

Laura plays the role of the victim in this drama. Like the virgins of the aristocratic Snilfards society on the planet Zycron, she falls prey to the barbaric rituals of the society in which she lives. Orphaned, raped, thinking her fetus aborted, she ultimately opts for suicide when all hope for rescue by her lover or her sister is gone. Laura seems to be a more rounded character than the Griffens. In part, this is because Atwood's readers come to know Laura both as she is described in Iris's reminiscences and as she seems to describe herself in what initially appears to be her semiautobiographical *The Blind Assassin*. At the moment when Atwood's readers realize that the unnamed woman of this novel within the novel is actually Iris rather than Laura (and this moment differs slightly, depending upon the particular reader), some confusion arises between two sisters. Inevitably, there is some overlap in readers' understanding of these characters in relation to the portrayal of the unnamed lover. In Iris's reminiscences, however, the distinction between the two sisters is quite clear. Laura is the heroine of the story that Iris scripts. Prone to idealized notions of death (evident first in her response to her mother's death, and later to her own suicide), committed to serving the needy (taking on the most difficult cases when working as an Abigail), and able to move outside the ranks of the aristocracy (as when she takes on a job at the waffle stand at Sunnyside and when she befriends and then helps Alex), Laura is a romantic.

Iris, in contrast to Laura, is a realist. The older of the two, she is motivated by duty rather than emotion. She marries for business reasons and remains married for financial reasons. As readers, though, we begin to assign worse motives to her as the novel progresses. We suspect that Iris is driven by competition and revenge rather than duty. After all, she strengthens her relationships with others (or perhaps it would be more accurate to say her hold on them) when she finds herself competing for them. Does she have an affair with Alex Thomas, for example, because Laura also wants him? Laura, judging from her response to the news of his death and unfaithfulness, feels deeply for him. We suspect, from the unnamed lover's refusal to leave her husband, that Iris does not feel quite the same depth of emotion. Similarly, Iris strengthens her ties with Aimee, her daughter, in response to her conflicts with Richard and Winifred. Aimee, herself, feels little for her mother. Indeed, she thinks that her mother is really Laura (assuming that Laura's fetus was not aborted), so much does she want to claim the romantic heroine as her next of kin. It is unclear whether Iris's granddaughter, Sabrina, would even recognize her.

Two things mitigate our harsh judgment of Iris as a villainess. First, she is herself a victim. Although she is one of the novel's blind assassins, she is also one of its sacrificed maidens. Surely her villainy is nothing more than the appropriate response to the monstrousness around her? Further, even with the tremendous strength she gathers during the course of her lifetime, it remains unclear whether she is entirely victorious. Like the others, she dies alone. Second, Iris's reminiscences as contained within the book that she pens for Sabrina read like a confession that is motivated by guilt and remorse. Here, Iris justifies her ruthlessness toward the Griffens, reveals the nature of her weapon (the novel known to the world as her sister's creation), and thereby testifies to the depths of her own creativity and imagination.

NARRATIVE STRUCTURE

There are three major narratives within this novel, each one telling a variation on the themes of blind assassin and sacrificed maiden. Indeed, the first two narratives essentially are the same story, told by the same person, but from such a different angle and with such a different focus that it is hard for the reader ever to see them as one and the same.

The frame text, or the narrative that seems to encapsulate the others within it, is narrated by Iris. This is the story of Iris's life, composed in a

public good, include Rahab who, in the Biblical tale, helps Joshua in the Fall of Jericho so as to save her family (part 8, "Carnivore Stories").

THEMES AND IMAGES

The novel's three epigraphs announce three of its dominant themes and set the dark tone of the novel. The first theme, of mass murder, emerges from a brief section of the English translation of Ryszard Kapuscinski's 1982 book, *Shah of Shahs,* which describes the horrific treatment of the city of Kerman at the hands of Agha Mohammed Khan, when he orders every citizen blinded or executed. Next, the theme of death as a kind of escape is implicit in the inscription taken from a Carthaginian funerary urn that describes a boundless sea and a merciless god as the answer to this speaker's prayers. Finally, the third epigraph announces the power of the word itself, which can be like a "flame burning in a dark glass" (a phrase taken from Canadian writer Sheila Watson's *Deep Hollow Creek*).

Within the novel, these three themes are shaped in terms of a series of images that, through repetition, gain the resonance of motifs. We come to understand, for example, that Iris is the mass murderer of this novel: that not only is her hand in each one of the crimes, but also her hand has scripted the way we understand those crimes. Perhaps it is not surprising that, in a novel about blind assassins who see through touch, hands gain a particular resonance. A disembodied hand appears on the margins of the Chase and Sons Labor Day picnic photo, indicating that the hand of the Chase sister not depicted in the photo itself is still in the events of the photo. As the image suggests, the two Chase sisters are never entirely independent of one another. However, each hand plays a slightly different role. The left hand is traditionally less dexterous than the right hand, and more gauche and sinister. Although more dexterous, the right hand is also the knife hand or, its equivalent here, the pen hand. As the novel unravels, Atwood's readers gain greater insight into which sister plays the role of which hand.

The second theme, of escape, is detailed through a number of different images. For those who commit suicide in this novel, death does indeed seem to be a kind of escape. But there are other forms of escape as well, involving flights into idealized romance, fantasy, or fiction. Romance, as foreshadowed by the image of the apple with which it is associated, proves an unsatisfactory form of escape. The afternoon of bliss under the apple tree of the Labor Day picnic, for example, is all too short-lived. Fantasy of the kind invented by the two lovers seems to be more satisfying. Indeed, it entertains the two of them during their affair, and its entertainment value is such that it earns the man some money when his typewriter transforms it into a book. Most effective of all escapes, however, is the fictional novel penned by Iris that serves her like the magician's box, becoming both the instrument of her crime and the means of her escape from her husband's tyranny.

Finally, the power of the word is enacted in a number of different ways in this novel. Individuals struggle to take control of the story, knowing that the individual in charge of life's script always has the upper hand. Richard wins control of the story of the hostile takeover of Chase Industries, but Iris wrests control of Laura's story. There is some suggestion, of course, that Iris wins a battle but not the whole war. As Lionel Warner points out in his article "Single Spies and Battalions," "It is an effectively subtle, post-feminist feature of the book that Iris begins life under the power of a Victorian father figure and ends reliant on Walter to perform manly tasks" (16). However, the passionate intensity of the flame to which Sheila Watson's epigraph alludes suggests the fascination that Laura and what the public assumes to be her novel hold for her audiences. Years after her death, fans come to her grave with flowers and notes, signaling that the flame of "her" vision has not been snuffed out. There are other flames in the novel as well. Laura colors the photograph of Richard so that flames appear behind his head. These are flames of passionate intensity, to be sure, but they are a destructive rather than a purifying or enlightening fire.

One other motif deserves mention because it is both pervasive and unusual. Buttons appear throughout the novel—as the source of the Chase family fortune, to be sure, but also as an image of something that stands at the point at which different pieces of material come together or move apart. Iris is, of course, herself the button in the various strands of this narrative.

AN INTERTEXTUAL READING

Intertextual readings examine the similarity between different works of literature. By comparing the text under scrutiny with a better-known or classic text, a reading can highlight some of the ways in which the author challenges the traditions that he or she has inherited and can locate some of the points upon which they differ markedly. It is precisely these points of contrast that prompt the most fruitful questions: about the rationale behind the contemporary author's decision to signal a comparison with and then deviate from the inherited script.

Atwood's *The Blind Assassin* signals its debt to numerous classics. The Chase girls' tutor, Mr. Erskine mentions Ovid, and one can recognize traces of his *Metamorphoses,* as the rapes of Europa by the bull, Leda by the swan, and Danae by a shower of gold reverberate with Iris's and Laura's experiences of abuse at the hands of powerful men (163). Also Iris's grandmother, Adelia, names the Chase family home "Avilion" after an island valley that appears in "The Passing of Arthur" section of *Idylls of the King* (a place "Where falls not hail, or rain, or any snow,/ Nor ever wind blows loudly; but it lies / Deep-meadow'd, happy, fair with orchard lawns / And bowery hollows crown'd with summer sea" (Tennyson 428–31). Readers can recognize: Romantic poet William Wordsworth's notion of "the inner eye that is the bliss of solitude" (part 5, "The Messenger"); Liu, a character in opera who commits suicide rather than betray her true love (part 5, "The Tango"); and Artemesia, the name of the Women's Press that republishes an edition of Laura Chase's novel and that might be named after three different Artemesias in history (part 7, "The Steamer Trunk"). Shelley Boyd also notes a parallel with Shakespeare's *King Lear* (also an important intertext for *Cat's Eye*). She writes in a note that deserves to be quoted at length:

> Atwood's novel seems to engage Shakespeare's *King Lear*. The father loses his empire, goes blind and dies imprisoned in his turret. I'm not sure if there is a Cordelia here or not. Laura and Iris seem closer to Goneril and Regan, who rival one another for Edmund, and eventually die. Goneril poisons Regan and later kills herself. On the surface, Laura and Iris clearly have less overt power than Goneril and Regan and seem to be dominated by men, rather than able to dominate them. Yet, in the end, Iris, in particular, reveals her subtle yet effective capabilities as a manipulator. If this parallel can be drawn, it would confirm that Atwood reverses our expectations about plot, and our assumptions about villainy. In Shakespeare, we do not like Goneril or Reagan, but support Cordelia. Yet in Atwood, Iris definitely has our sympathies, despite our discomfort with the lame way she accepts the arranged business-marriage contract her father devises and the way she uses her sister. (letter to author)

Of the four intertextual references I scrutinize here, the novel openly acknowledges the first two. References to the first of these, Coleridge's famous poem "Kubla Khan," appear a number of times during part 7 in the section entitled "Xanadu": first, when the Chase girls learn the poem from Miss Violence at Avilion; next, when the poem's first verse is used by Winifred on her invitations; and finally, when the Chase girls discuss the meaning of the poem together. Iris dons the costume of the Abyssinian maid of the poem. However, it is Laura who rightly decodes the message of the poem. She understands that Kubla Khan is to be feared because he is too happy. Who, then, is meant to be the Kubla Khan of Atwood's novel? Iris, by evading Laura's probes, shows herself unwilling to explore the possibilities. After all, like the Kubla Khan, by marrying the wealthy Richard Griffen, has she not already drunk "the milk of Paradise"? Is she not also to be feared?

The second acknowledged debt is to Virgil's classic epic (or serious work, written in an elevated style), the *Aeneid*. Once again, this is a text that the Chase girls have studied. Laura keeps the translation of a particularly poignant section at the epic's end, and, after Laura dies, Iris finds it in the notebooks Laura leaves her. The section details the role of Iris's namesake, the Iris sent by the powerful goddess Juno to ease Dido's agony as she lies dying from self-inflicted wounds after the wartime departure of her lover, Aeneas. In Atwood's novel, Alex clearly plays the role of Aeneas (in his wartime departure and untimely death), and Laura plays the role of Dido. At first glance, Atwood's Iris differs markedly from Virgil's. Atwood's Iris is blond, and she does not seem to have Laura's comfort in the top of her mind as she breaks the news of her affair with Alex and of his death to Laura at the restaurant called Diana Sweets. However, the ease brought by Iris to Dido is the ease of death, the severing of soul and body. Is this not precisely what Atwood's Iris achieves when she breaks the news to Laura? If so, then is Atwood suggesting that twentieth-century Ontario may not be such a far remove from the epic and momentous events of antiquity?

There are strong links to Greek as well as to Roman antiquity, although they are perhaps not so explicit. *The Blind Assassin* can be read as a modern-day retelling of such classic tragedies as Sophocles' *Electra* and, perhaps even more significantly, Sophocles' *Antigone*. Both tragedies are unusual in their focus on female heroines. They describe the effects of a daughter standing up for a cause, usually relating back to her father. Electra, with her brother, plots to kill her father's murderer, who is also her mother. Antigone speaks out against the injustice of the different burials of her two brothers—one who was buried with full honors, and the other buried in shame beyond the walls of the city—and goes so far as to perform a symbolic burial by sprinkling dust over the corpse. For her

Bibliography

WORKS BY MARGARET ATWOOD

Poetry

The Animals in That Country. Toronto: Oxford University Press, 1968.
The Circle Game. Toronto: Anansi, 1966.
Double Persephone. Toronto: Hawkshead Press, 1961.
Interlunar. Toronto: Oxford University Press, 1984.
The Journals of Susanna Moodie. Toronto: Oxford University Press, 1970.
Morning in the Burned House. Toronto: McClelland and Stewart, 1995.
Power Politics. Toronto: Anansi, 1971.
Procedures for Underground. Toronto: Oxford University Press, 1970.
True Stories. Toronto: Oxford University Press, 1981.
Two-Headed Poems. Toronto: Oxford University Press, 1978.
You Are Happy. Toronto: Oxford University Press, 1974.

Novels

Alias Grace. Toronto: McClelland and Stewart, 1996.
The Blind Assassin. Toronto: McClelland and Stewart, 2000.
Bodily Harm. Toronto: McClelland and Stewart, 1981.
Cat's Eye. Toronto: McClelland and Stewart, 1988.
The Edible Woman. Toronto: McClelland and Stewart, 1969.

The Handmaid's Tale. Toronto: McClelland and Stewart, 1985.
Lady Oracle. Toronto: McClelland and Stewart, 1976.
Life before Man. Toronto: McClelland and Stewart, 1979.
Oryx and Crake. Toronto: McClelland and Stewart, 2003.
The Robber Bride. Toronto: McClelland and Stewart, 1993.
Surfacing. Toronto: McClelland and Stewart, 1972.
"Up in the Air So Blue." Unpublished novel, 1963–64.

Short Fiction

Bluebeard's Egg. Toronto: McClelland and Stewart, 1983.
Bluebeard's Egg and Other Stories. New York: Fawcett Crest, 1987.
Dancing Girls and Other Stories. Toronto: McClelland and Stewart, 1977.
Good Bones. Toronto: Coach House Press, 1992.
Murder in the Dark: Short Fictions and Prose Poems. Toronto: Coach House Press,
    1983.
Wilderness Tips. Toronto: McClelland and Stewart, 1991.

Children's Fiction

Anna's Pet. Coauthored with Joyce Barkhouse. Illus. Ann Blades. Toronto: James
    Lorimer, 1980.
Up in the Tree. Toronto: McClelland and Stewart, 1978.

Criticism and Theory

Negotiating with the Dead: A Writer on Writing. New York: Cambridge University
    Press, 2002.
Second Words: Selected Critical Prose. Toronto: Anansi, 1982.
Strange Things: The Malevolent North in Canadian Literature. Oxford: Clarendon
    Press, 1995.
Survival: A Thematic Guide to Canadian Literature. Toronto: Anansi, 1972.

Other Works (Selected Articles, Plays, Librettos)

Barbed Lyres: Canadian Venomous Verse. Toronto: Key Porter Books, 1990.
"The Bombardment Continues." *Story of a Nation: Defining Moments in Our History.*
    Westwood Creative Artists and the Dominion Institute. Toronto: Double-
    day, 2001. 7–23.
"Bowering Pie . . . Some Recollections." *Essays on Canadian Writing* 38 (1989): 3–6.
"Case of the Crazed Cashier." *Toronto Life,* Mar. 1990: 46–47.
Days of the Rebels: 1815–1840. Toronto: Natural Science of Canada, 1977.
"Dennis Lee Revisited." *Descant* 39 (Winter 1982): 13–15.

"A Flying Start." *That Reminds Me: Canada's Authors Relive Their Most Embarrassing Moments.* Ed. Marta Kurc. Don Mills, Ontario: Stoddart, 1990. 11–13.

"Getting Out from Under." Address to the Empire Club of Canada. 15 Apr. 1973. Margaret Atwood Papers. University of Toronto. Box 56:19.

Margaret Atwood Papers. University of Toronto.

"Marie-Claire Blais Is Not for Burning." *Macleans,* Sept. 1975: 26, 28–29.

"On the Trail of Dashiell Hammett." *Globe and Mail,* 23 Feb. 2002: R1 and R7.

"Self-Discovery through Integration with One's Past." Shastri Institute Conference. 1988. Margaret Atwood Papers. University of Toronto. Box 148: 27.

The Servant Girl. CBC-TV, 1974.

"True North." *Saturday Night* 102.1 (Jan. 1987): 141–48.

The Trumpets of Summer. Music by John Beckwith. CBC Radio, 1964.

"Who Created Whom?" *New York Times Book Review,* 31 May 1987: 36.

"Why I Write." *Quill and Quire* 59.8 (Aug. 1993): 1, 21.

"Why I Write Poetry." *This Magazine,* Mar.–Apr. 1996: 44–48.

INTERVIEWS

Atwood, Margaret. "Dancing on the Edge of the Precipice." Interview with Joyce Carol Oates. *Margaret Atwood: Conversations.* Ed. Earl Ingersoll. Princeton, NJ: Ontario Review, 1990. 74–85.

———. "The Empress Has No Clothes." Interview with Elizabeth Meese. *Margaret Atwood: Conversations.* Ed. Earl Ingersoll. Princeton, NJ: Ontario Review, 1990. 177–90.

———. "Margaret Atwood." Interview with Graeme Gibson. *Eleven Canadian Novelists.* Toronto: Anansi, 1973. 5–31.

———. Personal interview with author. 1 May 1996.

———. "Using Other People's Dreadful Childhoods." Interview with Bonnie Lyons. *Margaret Atwood: Conversations.* Ed. Earl Ingersoll. Princeton, NJ: Ontario Review, 1990. 221–33.

———. "Witch Craft." Interview with Camille Peri. *Mother Jones,* Apr. 1989: 28–33.

———. "Witness Is What You Must Bear." Interview with Beatrice Mendez-Egle. *Margaret Atwood: Conversations.* Ed. Earl Ingersoll. Princeton, NJ: Ontario Review, 1990. 162–70.

Ford, James. Telephone interview with author. 23 Jan. 1998, 9 June 1998.

Lloyd, Chris. Telephone interview with author. 26 Apr. 1996.

Pachter, Charles. Personal interview with author. 8 Sept. 1995.

———. Personal interview with author. 4 Nov. 1997.

LETTERS

Atwood, Margaret. Letter to Charles Pachter. 28 Dec. 1968. Private Collection.

———. Letter to Pierre Castonguay. 20 Feb. 1984. Margaret Atwood Papers. University of Toronto. Box 74: 15. Author's translation.

————. Letter to the author. 26 Aug. 1995.
————. Letter to the author. 28 Nov. 1995.
Bingley, Xandra. Letter to the author. 21 May 1996.
Boyd, Shelley. Letter to the author. 21 July 2003.
Cogswell, Kay. Letter to the author. 26 Jan. 1998.
Sims, Mary. Letter to the author. 2 Apr. 1996.
Verkade, Rachel. Letter to the author. 18 March 2003.
Zurbrigg, Terri. Letter to the author. 1 Oct. 2002.

BIOGRAPHICAL INFORMATION

Cooke, Nathalie. "Lions, Tigers, and Pussycats: Margaret Atwood [Auto-]Bio-
    graphically." *Margaret Atwood: Works and Impact.* Ed. Reingard M. Nischik.
    European Studies in American Literature and Culture Series. Rochester, NY:
    Camden House, 2000. 15–27.
————. *Margaret Atwood: A Biography.* Toronto: ECW Press, 1998.
Sullivan, Rosemary. *The Red Shoes: Margaret Atwood, Starting Out.* Toronto:
    HarperFlamingo Publishers, 1998.

REVIEWS AND CRITICISM

The Blind Assassin

Bemrose, John. "Margaret's Museum." Rev. of *The Blind Assassin,* by Margaret
    Atwood. *Maclean's,* 11 Sept. 2000: 54–56.
"New Fiction Hand-and-I Co-Ordination." Rev. of *The Blind Assassin*, by Margaret
    Atwood. *The Economist,* 30 Sept. 2000: no page number.
Smith, Stephen. "*The Blind Assassin.*" Rev. of *The Blind Assassin*, by Margaret At-
    wood. *Quill and Quire* 66 (2000): 21.
Warner, Lionel. "Single Spies and Battalions." *English Review* 12.1 (Sept. 2001): 16.
Wilson, Sharon R. "Margaret Atwood and Popular Culture: *The Blind Assassin* and
    Other Novels." *Journal of American and Comparative Cultures* 25.3–4 (2002):
    270–76.

Cat's Eye

Cooke, Nathalie. "The Politics of Ventriloquism: Margaret Atwood's Fictive Con-
    fessions." *Various Atwoods.* Ed. Lorraine York. Toronto: Anansi, 1995. 207–28.
Fulford, Robert. "Kernel of Glass at the Heart of New Atwood Heroine. Rev. of
    Cat's Eye, by Margaret Atwood. *Quill and Quire* 54 (Oct. 1988): 18.
Kanfer, Stefan. "Time Arrested." Rev. of *Cat's Eye*, by Margaret Atwood. *Time*, 6
    Feb. 1989: 70.
Stuewe, Paul. "Intensely Experienced, Profoundly Engrossing." Rev. of *Cat's Eye*,
    by Margaret Atwood. *Toronto Star* 21 Oct. 1989: M14.

The Edible Woman

Bell, Millicent. "The Girl on the Wedding Cake: *The Edible Woman*." Rev. of *The Edible Woman*, by Margaret Atwood. *New York Times* 18 Oct. 1970: BR26.

MacLulich, T. D. "Atwood's Adult Fairy Tale: Levi-Strauss, Bettelheim, and *The Edible Woman*." *Essays on Canadian Writing* 11 (1978): 111–29.

Montagnes, Anne. "Two Novels That Unveil, Maybe, a Coming Phenomenon, the Species Torontonensis." Rev. of *The Edible Woman*, by Margaret Atwood. *Saturday Night* 84 (Nov. 1969): 54, 56 + .

Skelton, Robin. Review of *The Edible Woman*. *Malahat Review*, no. 13 (January 1970), pg. 108–109.

Stedmond, John. "*The Edible Woman*." Rev. of *The Edible Woman*, by Margaret Atwood. *The Canadian Forum* 49 (1970): 267.

The Handmaid's Tale

Barbé Hammer, Stephanie. "'The World as It Will Be?' Female Satire and the Technology of Power in *The Handmaid's Tale*." *Modern Language Studies* 20.2 (1990): 39–49.

Blaise, Clark. "Atwood Fires Poisoned Valentine at U.S. Males: High Priestess of CanLit Creates Anti-Utopia where Women Are Powerless, Pregnant, Poor." Rev. of *The Handmaid's Tale*, by Margaret Atwood. *Gazette* 5 Oct. 1985: B7.

Ehrenreich, Barbara. Rev. of *The Handmaid's Tale*, by Margaret Atwood. *New Republic*, 17 Mar. 1986: 33 + .

Glendinning, Victoria. Rev. of *The Handmaid's Tale*, by Margaret Atwood. *Saturday Night* 181 (Jan. 1986): 39–41.

Lehmann-Haupt, Christopher. "Books of the Times." Rev. of *The Handmaid's Tale*, by Margaret Atwood. *New York Times* 27 Jan. 1986: C24.

Wilson, Sharon R. "Introduction." *Approaches to Teaching Atwood's* The Handmaid's Tale *and Other Works*. Ed. Thomas B. Friedman, Shannon Hengen, and Sharon R. Wilson. NewYork: Modern Language Association of America, 1996. 23–27.

York, Lorraine. "Satire: The No-Woman's Land of Literary Modes." *Approaches to Teaching Atwood's* The Handmaid's Tale *and Other Works*. Eds. Thomas Friedman, Shannon Hengen, and Sharon Wilson. New York: Modern Language Association of America, 1996. 43–48.

Lady Oracle

Brophy, Brigid. "A Contrary Critic Takes a Crack at *Lady Oracle*." *Globe and Mail* 9 Oct. 1976, pg. 33.

Duffy, Dennis. "Read for Its Gracefulness, for Its Good Story, for Its Help in Your Fantasy Life." Rev. of *Lady Oracle*, by Margaret Atwood. *Globe and Mail* 4 Sept. 1976: 32.

Pollitt, Katha. *"Lady Oracle."* Rev. of *Lady Oracle*, by Margaret Atwood. *New York Times* 26 Sept. 1976: BR2.

Oryx and Crake

Richler, Noah. "Atwood's Ground Zero: Like Her Earlier *The Handmaid's Tale;* Margaret Atwood's Latest Novel, *Oryx and Crake*, is set in a Dystopian Future. But, as the Author Explains, the Perils Are All Too Familiar." *National Post* 26 Apr. 2003: BK1.

Surfacing

Campbell, Josie P. "The Woman as Hero in Margaret Atwood's *Surfacing.*" *Mosaic* 11.3 (Spring 1978): 17–28.

Clery, Val. "A Plea for the Victims." *Books in Canada* 1.12 (Nov.–Dec. 1972): 45–46.

Delany, Paul. *"Surfacing."* Rev. of *Surfacing*, by Margaret Atwood. *New York Times* 4 Mar. 1973: 441.

Elliot, Gordon R. Review of *The Edible Woman*. *West Coast Reviews* 5, no. 2 (October 1970): 68–69.

Fraser, D. M. "Margaret Atwood's *Surfacing*: Some Notes." 3 *Pulp* 2.7 (1 May 1974) 1–4.

French, William. "Exhilarating: An All-Purpose Novel." Rev. of *Surfacing*, by Margaret Atwood. *Globe and Mail* 16 Sept. 1972: 30.

Harcourt, Joan. "Atwood Country." *Queen's Quarterly* 80.2 (Summer 1973): 278–81.

Harrison, James. "The 20,000,000 Solitudes of Surfacing." *Dalhousie Review* 59 (1979): 74–81.

King, Bruce. "Margaret Atwood's *Surfacing.*" *Journal of Commonwealth Literature* 12.1 (Aug. 1977): 23–32.

Kokotailo, Philip. "Form in Atwood's *Surfacing*. Toward a Synthesis of Critical Opinion." *Studies in Canadian Literature* 8.2 (1983): 155–65.

Lehmann-Haupt, Christopher. "Novels with Anxious Moments." Rev. of *Surfacing*, by Margaret Atwood. *New York Times* 7 Mar. 1973: 41.

Pratt, Annis. *"Surfacing* and the Rebirth Journey." *The Art of Margaret Atwood: Essays in Criticism.* Ed. Arnold E. Davidson and Cathy N. Davidson. Toronto: Anansi, 1981. 139–57.

Rubenstein, Roberta. *"Surfacing:* Margaret Atwood's Journey to the Interior." *Modern Fiction Studies* 22.3 (Autumn 1976): 387–99.

OTHER ATWOOD CRITICISM

Brown, Russell. "Atwood's Sacred Wells." *Essays on Canadian Writing* 17 (Spring 1980): 5–43.

Davison, Carol. "Margaret Atwood." *Gothic Writers: A Critical and Bibliographical*

Guide. Ed. Douglass H. Thomson, Jack G. Voller, and Frederick S. Frank. Westport, CT: Greenwood, 2002. 24–32.

Howells, Coral Ann. *Margaret Atwood.* New York: St. Martin's Press, 1996.

Jonas, George. "Canada Discovers Its 'Thing.'" *Macleans,* 25 Dec.–1 Jan. 1995: 63.

Lyons, Bonnie. "'Neither Victims Nor Executioners' in Margaret Atwood's Fiction." *World Literature Written in English* 17.1 (Apr. 1978): 181–87.

Mandel, Eli. "Atwood Gothic." *Malahat Review* 41 (Jan. 1977): 165–74.

Nischik, Reingard. "Margaret Atwood in Statements by Fellow Writers." *Margaret Atwood: Works and Impact.* Rochester, NY: Camden House, 2000. 305–10.

Once in August. Dir. Michael Rubbo. NFB, 1984.

Patnaik, Eira. "The Succulent Gender: Eat Her Softly." *Literary Gastronomy.* Ed. David Bevan. Amsterdam: Rodopi, 1988. 59–76.

Rosenberg, Jerome. *Margaret Atwood.* Boston: Twayne Publishers, 1984.

Wilson, Sharon R. *Margaret Atwood's Fairy-Tale Sexual Politics.* Jackson: University of Mississippi Press, 1993.

Woodcock, George. "Transformation Mask for Margaret Atwood." *Malahat Review* 41 (1977): 52–56.

WORKS OF GENERAL INTEREST

Abrams, M. H. *Glossary of Literary Terms.* 4th ed. New York: Holt, Rinehart and Winston, 1981.

Albee, Edward. *Who's Afraid of Virginia Woolf?* New York: Atheneum, 1962.

Aristotle. *Poetics.* Trans. Leon Golden. *The Critical Tradition: Classic Texts and Contemporary Trends.* Ed. David Richter. New York: St. Martin's Press, 1989. 42–65.

Austen, Jane. *Northanger Abbey.* 1818. Ed. Claire Grogan. 2nd ed. Peterborough, Ontario: Broadview Press, 2002.

Barkhouse, Joyce [Joan]. *Pit Pony.* Toronto: Gage Educational, 1990.

Barth, John. *Lost in the Funhouse: Fiction for Print, Tape, Live Voice.* Garden City, NY: Doubleday, 1968.

Baudrillard, Jean. *Simulations.* Trans. Paul Foss, Paul Patton, and Philip Beitchman. New York: Semiotext(e), 1983.

Bloom, Harold. *The Anxiety of Influence: A Theory of Poetry.* 2nd ed. New York: Oxford University Press, 1997.

Bolster, Stephanie. *White Stone: The Alice Poems.* Montreal: Signal Editions, Véhicule Press, 1998.

Bowering, George. *The Gangs of Kosmos.* Toronto: Anansi, 1969.

Brontë, Emily. *Wuthering Heights.* 1847. Ed. Ian Jack. New York: Oxford University Press, 1981.

Brooke, Frances. *The History of Emily Montague.* 1769. Ottawa: Carleton University Press, 1985.

Brothers Grimm. *The Complete Grimm's Fairy Tales.* New York: Pantheon, 1972.

Brown, Russell. "In Search of Lost Causes: The Canadian Novelist as Mystery Writer." *Mosaic* 11.3 (Spring 1978): 1–15.

————. "Theme." *Encyclopedia of Contemporary Literary Theory.* Ed. Irene Makaryk. Toronto: University of Toronto Press, 1993: 642–46.

Buckley, Jerome Hamilton. *Season of Youth: The Bildungsroman from Dickens to Golding.* Cambridge, MA: Harvard University Press, 1974.

Carroll, Lewis. *Alice in Wonderland.* Toronto: John C. Winston, 1952.

Chaucer, Geoffrey. *The Works of Geoffrey Chaucer.* Ed. F. N. Robinson. London: Oxford University Press, 1957.

Chopin, Kate. *The Awakening.* 1899. New York: Simon and Schuster, 1996.

Coleridge, Samuel Taylor. "Kubla Kahn." 1816. *Norton Anthology of Poetry.* Shorter 4th ed. Ed. Margaret Ferguson, Mary Jo Salter, and Jon Stallworthy. New York: Norton, 1997. 428–29.

Colombo, John Robert, and Jacques Godbout. *Poésie/Poetry 64.* Montreal: Editions du jour; Toronto: Ryerson Press, 1963.

Crozier, Lorna. *The Garden Going On Without Us.* Toronto: McClelland and Stewart, 1985.

————. *A Saving Grace: The Collected Poems of Mrs. Bentley.* Toronto: McClelland and Stewart, 1996.

De Bruyn, Frans. "Genre Criticism." *Encyclopedia of Contemporary Literary Theory.* Ed. Irene Makaryk. Toronto: University of Toronto Press, 1993. 79–85.

Derrida, Jacques. *Writing and Difference.* Trans. Alan Bass. Chicago: University of Chicago Press, 1978.

————. *Speech and Phenomena.* Trans. David B. Allison. Evanston, IL: Northwestern University Press, 1973.

Dickens, Charles. *Great Expectations.* 1860. Ed. Emma Holden. Harlow, England: Longman, 1991.

Donleavy, J. P. *The Ginger Man.* New York: Delacorte, 1965.

DuPlessis, Rachel Blau. *Writing Beyond the Ending: Narrative Strategies of Twentieth Century Women Writers.* Bloomington: Indiana University Press, 1985.

Eliot, T. S. "Tradition and the Individual Talent." *Selected Essays.* 1932. Boston: Faber and Faber, 1980. 13–22.

Engel, Marian. *Bear: A Novel.* Toronto: McClelland and Stewart, 1976.

Faulkner, William. *Absalom! Absalom!* 1936. New York: Random House, 1936.

————. *As I Lay Dying.* 1930. New York: Random House, 1964.

————. *Sanctuary.* 1931. New York: Random House, 1958.

————. *The Sound and the Fury.* 1956. New York: Random House. 1956.

Flax, Jane. "The Conflict Between Nurturance & Autonomy in Mother-Daughter Relationships within Feminism." *Feminist Studies* 4 (June 1978): 171–89

Fowler, Alistair. *Kinds of Literature: An Introduction to the Theory of Genres and Modes.* Cambridge: Harvard University Press, 1982.

Friedan, Betty. *The Feminine Mystique.* 1963. New York: Dell, 1964.

Frye, Northrop. *The Bush Garden: Essays on the Canadian Imagination*. Toronto: Anansi, 1971.

Galeano, Eduardo. *Memory of Fire: Genesis*. 1982. Trans. Cedric Belfrage. New York: Pantheon, 1985.

Gibson, Graeme. *Five Legs*. Toronto: Anansi, 1969.

Gibson, Shirley. *I Am Watching*. Toronto: Anansi, 1973.

Gilbert, Sandra, and Susan Gubar. *The Madwoman in the Attic: The Woman Writer and the Nineteenth-Century Literary Imagination*. New Haven, CT: Yale University Press, 1984.

Gilman, Charlotte Perkins. "The Yellow Wallpaper." 1892. *The Yellow Wallpaper*. Ed. Thomas L. Erskine and Connie L. Richards. New Brunswick, NJ: Rutgers University Press, 1993. 29–50.

Godfrey, Ellen. *The Case of the Cold Murderer*. Toronto: Anansi, 1976.

"gorgon." *Oxford English Dictionary Online*. 2nd ed. 2003. Oxford University Press. 17 July 2003. <http://www.dictionary.oed.com>.

Graham, Gwethalyn. *Swiss Sonata*. New York: Charles Scribner's Sons, 1938.

Grant, George. *Technology and Empire: Perspectives on North America*. Toronto: Anansi, 1969.

Graves, Robert. *The White Goddess: A Historical Grammar of Poetic Myth*. 1948. New York: Octagon Books, 1972.

Hardy, Thomas. *Jude the Obscure*. 1895. New York: Harper, 1957.

Hemingway, Ernest. "Hills like White Elephants." *The Complete Short Stories of Ernest Hemingway*. Ed. Finca Vigia. New York: Scribner's, 1987. 211–14.

Henighan, Stephen. *When Words Deny the World: The Reshaping of Canadian Writing*. Erin, Ontario: Porcupine's Quill, 2002.

Hite, Molly. *The Other Side of the Story: Structure and Strategies of Contemporary Feminist Narrative*. Ithaca: Cornell University Press, 1989.

Hutcheon, Linda. *The Canadian Postmodern: A Study in Contemporary Canadian Fiction*. Don Mill, Ontario: Oxford University Press, 1988.

James, Henry. *The Jolly Corner*. 1909. Ed. Roger Gard. London: Penguin, 1990.

———. *Turn of the Screw*. 1898. Ed. Peter E. Beidler. Boston: Bedford, 1995.

Joyce, James. *A Portrait of the Artist as a Young Man*. 1916. New York: Viking Press, 1964.

Kapuscinski, Ryszard. *Shah of Shahs*. New York: Harcourt Brace, 1982.

Kerouac, Jack. *On the Road*. Harmondsworth: Penguin Books, 1976.

Klein, A. M. "Portrait of the Poet as Landscape." *The Rocking Chair and Other Poems*. Toronto: Ryerson Press, 1966. 55.

Kroetsch, Robert. *Badlands: a Novel*. Toronto: New Press, 1975.

———. *Labyrinths of Voice: Conversations with Robert Kroetsch*. Ed. Shirley Neuman and Robert Wilson. Edmonton: NeWest Press, 1982.

———. "Unhiding the Hidden: Recent Canadian Fiction." *Journal of Canadian Fiction* 3.3 (1974): 43–45.

MacEwen, Gwendolyn. *Shadow-Maker.* Toronto: Macmillan, 1972.

Laurence, Margaret. *The Diviners.* Toronto: McClelland and Stewart, 1974.

———. *The Stone Angel.* Toronto: McClelland and Stewart, 1964.

Lawrence, D. H. *Sons and Lovers.* 1913. New York: Cambridge University Press, 1992.

Leacock, Stephen. *Sunshine Sketches of a Little Town.* 1912. Toronto: McClelland and Stewart, 1989.

Lecker, Robert. *Making it Real: The Canonization of English-Canadian Literature.* Concord, Ontario: Anansi, 1995.

Lee, Dennis. *Civil Elegies and Other Poems.* Toronto: Anansi, 1972.

Lessing, Doris. *The Golden Notebook.* 1962. St. Albans: Panther, 1973.

Lewis, Matthew. *The Monk: A Romance.* 1797. London: George Routledge and Sons, 1929.

Lyotard, Jean-François. *The Postmodern Condition: A Report on Knowledge.* Trans. Geoff Bennington and Brian Massumi. Minneapolis: University of Minnesota Press, 1984.

Montgomery, L. M. *Anne of Green Gables.* New York: Bantam Books, 1976.

———. *The Blue Castle: A Novel.* Toronto: McClelland and Stewart, 1994.

Munro, Alice. *Lives of Girls and Women.* Toronto: McGraw-Hill Ryerson, 1971.

———. "Something I've Been Meaning to Tell You." *Something I've Been Meaning to Tell You . . . Thirteen Stories.* Toronto: McGraw-Hill Ryerson, 1974. 1–19.

New, William H. *A History of Canadian Literature.* New York: New Amsterdam Books, 1989.

Ondaatje, Michael. *Coming through the Slaughter.* Toronto: Anansi, 1976.

———. *In the Skin of a Lion.* Toronto: McClelland and Stewart, 1987.

Orwell, George. *Animal Farm.* 1945. New York: Harcourt, Brace, 1946.

Ovid. *Metamorphoses.* Trans. A. D. Melville. Oxford: Oxford University Press, 1986.

Plato. *Republic*, Book 10. Trans. Benjamin Jowett. *The Critical Tradition: Classic Texts and Contemporary Trends.* Ed. David Richter. New York: St. Martin's Press, 1989. 21–29.

Pynchon, Robert. *Gravity's Rainbow.* New York: Viking Press, 1973.

Radcliffe, Ann. *The Mysteries of Udolpho.* 1794. New York: Oxford University Press, 1998.

Radway, Janice. *Reading the Romance: Women, Patriarchy, and Popular Literature.* Chapel Hill: University of North Carolina Press, 1984.

Rich, Adrienne. "Diving in the Wreck." 1972. *Diving in the Wreck: Poems 1971–1972.* New York: Norton, 1973. 22–24.

Richler, Mordecai. *The Apprenticeship of Duddy Kravitz.* 1959. Toronto: Emblem Editions, 2001.

———. *St. Urbain's Horseman.* New York: Knopf, 1971.

Rooke, Constance. *Fear of the Open Heart: Essays on Contemporary Canadian Writing.* Toronto: Couch House Press, 1989.

Roy, Gabrielle. *Bonheur d'occasion.* Montreal: Société des Editions Pascal, 1945.

Saussure, Ferdinand de. *Cours de Linguistique Générale.* Ed. Charles Bailley and Albert Sechehaye in collaboration with Albert Riedlinger. Paris: Payot, 1931.

Schellenberg, Elizabeth, "Reader-Response Criticism," *Encyclopedia of Contemporary Literary Theory.* Ed. Irene Makaryk. Toronto: University of Toronto Press, 1993. 170–73.

Shakespeare, William. *The Tragedy of King Lear. The Riverside Shakespeare.* Boston: Houghton Mifflin, 1974. 1255–305.

———. *The Tragedy of Macbeth. The Riverside Shakespeare.* Boston: Houghton Mifflin, 1974. 1312–42.

Shelley, Mary. *Frankenstein.* 1817. Ed. Richard Anobile. New York: Universe Books, 1974.

Shields, Carol. *The Stone Diaries.* Toronto: Vintage, 1993.

Smith, Donald A. *At the Forks of the Grand: Twenty Historical Essays on Paris, Ontario.* [Paris]: Walker Press, 1950.

Sophocles. *Antigone.* Trans. Reginald Gibbons and Charles Segal. Oxford: Oxford University Press, 2003.

———. *Electra.* Ed. and Trans. Jenny March. Warminster: Aris and Phillips, 2001.

Stevens, Wallace. "Autumn Refrain." *The Collected Poems.* New York: Random House; New York: Vintage Books, 1923. 60.

Sullivan, Rosemary. *Shadow Maker: The Life of Gwendolyn MacEwen.* Toronto: HarperCollins, 1995.

Swift, Jonathan. *Gulliver's Travels.* 1726. New York: Oxford University Press, 1977.

Tennyson, Alfred Lord. "The Lady of Shalott." 1842. *Tennyson's Poems.* T. Y. Crowell, 1876.

———. "The Passing of Arthur." 1869. *Idylls of the King.* Ed. J. M. Gray. New Haven, CT: Yale University Press, 1983. 288–300.

Van Eyck, Johannes. *The Arnolfini Marriage.* National Gallery, London.

Virgil. *Aeneid.* Trans. Robert Fitzgerald. New York: Random, 1983.

Walpole, Horace. *The Castle of Otranto.* 1764. London: Grey Walls Press, 1950.

Watson, Sheila. *Deep Hollow Creek.* Toronto: McClelland and Stewart, 1992.

———. *The Double Hook.* 1966. Toronto: McClelland and Stewart, 1989.

Waugh, Patricia. *Metafiction: The Theory and Practice of Self-Conscious Fiction.* London, New York: Methuen, 1984.

Wordsworth, William. "I Wandered Lonely As a Cloud." *Poems, in Two Volumes.* London: Longman, Hurst, Rees, and Orme, 1807.

Woolf, Virginia. *A Room of One's Own.* [1929. San Diego] London: Hogarth Press; New York: Fountain Press; New York: Harcourt Brace, 1929.

Index

Woman. *See* Female characters
Women's rights, 11, 79
Woodcock, George, 25
Woolf, Virginia, 23, 70
Word theme, power of, 150, 151
Writing(s): challenging conventions of, 29; as a dark art, 16–18; rules of, 29; technique (*see* Writing techniques); as theme, 79; themes of, 11

Writing techniques: bringing history to life, 2; making current issues personal, 1–2; of *Surfacing*, 2; using personal point of view, 2; using the first-person, 2, 69, 98; weaving the dark mysteries of fiction, 3. *See also* Satire

York, Lorraine, 114

The author gratefully acknowledges the support of a research grant from the Social Sciences and Humanities Research Council of Canada; and the invaluable research assistance of Shelley Boyd and Terri Susan Zurbrigg.

About the Author

Nathalie Cooke is Associate Professor of English at McGill University in Montreal. She is the author of *Margaret Atwood: A Biography* and she has authored and edited several books on Canadian Literature and Poetry.

Critical Companions to Popular Contemporary Writers
First Series—also available on CD-ROM

V. C. Andrews *by E. D. Huntley*

Tom Clancy *by Helen S. Garson*

Mary Higgins Clark *by Linda C. Pelzer*

Arthur C. Clarke *by Robin Anne Reid*

James Clavell *by Gina Macdonald*

Pat Conroy *by Landon C. Burns*

Robin Cook *by Lorena Laura Stookey*

Michael Crichton *by Elizabeth A. Trembley*

Howard Fast *by Andrew Macdonald*

Ken Follett *by Richard C. Turner*

John Grisham *by Mary Beth Pringle*

James Herriot *by Michael J. Rossi*

Tony Hillerman *by John M. Reilly*

John Jakes *by Mary Ellen Jones*

Stephen King *by Sharon A. Russell*

Dean Koontz *by Joan G. Kotker*

Robert Ludlum *by Gina Macdonald*

Anne McCaffrey *by Robin Roberts*

Colleen McCullough *by Mary Jean DeMarr*

James A. Michener *by Marilyn S. Severson*

Anne Rice *by Jennifer Smith*

Tom Robbins *by Catherine E. Hoyser and Lorena Laura Stookey*

John Saul *by Paul Bail*

Erich Segal *by Linda C. Pelzer*

Gore Vidal *by Susan Baker and Curtis S. Gibson*